ENTREPRENEURSHIP AND EMOTIONS

ENTREPRENEURSHIP AND EMOTIONS: INSIGHTS ON VENTURE PERFORMANCE

BY

SARA SASSETTI

University of Pisa, Italy

United Kingdom – North America – Japan – India
Malaysia – China

Emerald Publishing Limited
Howard House, Wagon Lane, Bingley BD16 1WA, UK

First edition 2021

Reprints and permissions service
Contact: permissions@emeraldinsight.com

British Library Cataloguing in Publication Data
A catalogue record for this book is available from the British Library

ISBN: 978-1-80117-355-1 (Print)
ISBN: 978-1-80117-354-4 (Online)
ISBN: 978-1-80117-356-8 (Epub)

Printed and bound by CPI Group (UK) Ltd, Croydon, CR0 4YY

ISOQAR certified
Management System,
awarded to Emerald
for adherence to
Environmental
standard
ISO 14001:2004.

ISOQAR
REGISTERED
Certificate Number 1985
ISO 14001

INVESTOR IN PEOPLE

Dedication

To my family, the reason why I always think positive

CONTENTS

ABOUT THE AUTHOR

Sara Sassetti is an Assistant Professor of Organizational Studies at the University of Pisa. She received her PhD in Management in 2018 from the University of Pisa, Economics and Management Department. Her main research field relates to entrepreneurial decision-making, students' employability and HRM. She works and collaborates with Southampton Business School. She is a Member of European Academy of Management (EURAM) and Track Chair for the EURAM entrepreneurship standing track 'Entrepreneurial Decision Making and Behavior'.

ACKNOWLEDGEMENTS

I would like to thank the European Academy of Management community and the scholars at the SIG of Entrepreneurship; while there, I had the opportunity to increase my knowledge and curiosity about the world of entrepreneurship and mostly to discuss my research topic with colleagues and friends. In particular, I would like to express my gratitude to Andrea and Massimiliano for involving me in this important research community.

Thank you to my friends Marco, Martina, and Sara; during these last months, in the middle of a pandemic, your support in our 'social control' virtual room has been invaluable.

A special thank you to my Mentor, Professor Vincenzo Cavaliere, who always supports me even when he does not agree with my point of view.

Finally, sincere appreciation goes to my family, who have always supported my decisions and cheered me on. To my father, who has all of an entrepreneur's virtues and vices. Three years later, I am sure that you are close to realising all your innovative ideas. To my mother, cornerstone of our family. To my precious brothers, Federico e Francesco, who always remind me how crazy, funny, and great our family is.

INTRODUCTION

Recent research efforts (e.g. Baron, 2008; Ingram, Peake, Stewart, & Watson, 2019; Lerner, Valdesolo, & Kassam, 2015) have underlined the necessity of considering emotions during discussions of entrepreneurial performance. Indeed, the latest studies have argued that entrepreneurial emotion is an 'hot topic' (Cardon, Foo, Shepherd, & Wiklund, 2012); accordingly, research shows that emotions influence both opportunity evaluation and exploitation decision (Hayton & Cholakova, 2012; Welpe, Spörrle, Grichnik, Michl, & Audretsch, 2012) and performance in general (Baron, Hmieleski, & Henry, 2012; Cardon, Wincent, Singh, & Drnovsek, 2009). This is due to the fact that 'entrepreneurship generates substantial emotions because it is an extreme context in terms of time pressures, uncertainty, and the extent of personal consequences tied up in the fate of the firm' (Cardon et al., 2012, p. 7).

For these reasons, this book aims to emphasise that entrepreneurship is a high emotional labour context, where positive and negative affect have a critical role and where emotions have to be controlled in order to achieve better performance (Cardon et al., 2012). Although scholars have begun to emphasise the role of emotion in entrepreneurial behaviour, including how positive affect influences entrepreneurs' engagement and performance (Baron et al., 2012; Cardon et al., 2009), this line of inquiry still needs to be understood in a more overarching manner (Ingram et al., 2019).

To better understand the role of emotions in entrepreneurship, the areas of focus are positive and negative affect and emotional intelligence. Entrepreneurial affect refers to the emotions, moods, or feelings of entrepreneurs that accompany the entire process of entrepreneurship (Cardon et al., 2012). As an important psychological feature of such individuals, it plays an important role in optimising entrepreneurial cognitive ability, inducing entrepreneurial behaviour, and subsequently affecting entrepreneurial performance (Baron & Tang, 2011; Dijkhuizen, Gorgievski, van Veldhoven, & Schalk, 2016). In the same vein, according to Salovey and Mayer (1990, p. 189), emotional intelligence is defined as 'the ability to monitor one's own and others' feelings, to discriminate among them, and to use this information to guide one's thinking and action'. In this definition, emotions are considered as 'useful sources of information that help one to make sense of and navigate the social environment' (Salovey & Grewal, 2005, p. 281). Moreover, in the decision-making process, if a person is able to understand his/her own emotions this allows him/her to realise not only the motivations at the base of decisions but also the potential consequences of those decisions for others (Hess & Bacigalupo, 2011). Following the argument that emotional intelligence plays an important role in affecting the decision-making process (Hess & Bacigalupo, 2013), emotional intelligence could help distinguish good performers (i.e. entrepreneurs) from bad performers (Boyatzis, 2009; Goleman, 1998).

Starting from these theoretical premises, the intention of this book is to contribute to entrepreneurship literature explaining and summarising how affect, both positive and negative, and the emotional intelligence of entrepreneurs have an impact on venture performance. In order to achieve this aim, the first chapter focuses on the understanding of the relationship between affect and entrepreneurship. After explaining that the literature about affect and entrepreneurship can be classified following four main criteria – the level of analysis, the antecedents and consequences of affect, the consequences of affect for the entrepreneurial process, and the facets of affect analysed (Delgado García, De Quevedo Puente, & Blanco Mazagatos, 2015) – a focus on the main literature about the relationship between positive and negative affect and venture performance is provided.

In Chapter 2, the main topic is an investigation of the role of emotional intelligence in entrepreneurship field. As with Chapter 1, the main contributions involving this topic will be discussed. Using this literature review as a base, Chapter 3 presents some hypotheses and explains the related theoretical framework to be tested. The second part of the chapter focuses on explaining the research method adopted to test the theoretical framework, while also describing the data collection, the research setting, and the sample. Specifically, the aim of this research is to investigate the emotional side of venture performance; in order to do so, the hypotheses which composed the theoretical framework consider positive and negative affect and emotional intelligence and explain how these emotional components should be related to entrepreneurs' venture performance.

Consequently, Chapter 4 aims to describe the empirical analysis conducted in order to test the theoretical framework. The descriptive statistics, considering the minimum and maximum value for each variable investigated and the related mean and standard deviation, are described; in addition, the correlation matrix results are presented. Subsequently, confirmatory factor analysis (CFA) is performed and finally the results of regression analysis run using SPSS v.26 are reported. In the final chapter, the main findings regarding the emotional side of venture performance are discussed and the theoretical and practical implications are presented.

1

UNDERSTANDING THE RELATIONSHIP BETWEEN AFFECT AND ENTREPRENEURSHIP

1.1 AFFECT AND ENTREPRENEURSHIP: SOME DEFINITIONS

Melissa Cardon, one of the most important researchers with regard to the role of affect and emotions in the field of entrepreneurship, together with other colleagues, stated that 'entrepreneurship generates substantial emotions because it is an extreme context in terms of time pressures, uncertainty, and the extent of personal consequences tied up in the fate of the firm' (Cardon et al., 2012, p. 1). Indeed, there are several reasons why affect may be relevant for entrepreneurs (Baron, 2015). First, as underlined by Cardon and colleagues, entrepreneurs often operate in highly uncertain and dynamic environments and their behaviours and actions are mostly influenced by unpredictable and ambiguous contexts. In these situations the emotional side is often the dominant characteristic when decisions have to be made and strategies have to be applied. Second, persons who want to be entrepreneurs are often able to experience intense affect and emotions. Indeed, entrepreneurs are often described as having high levels of passion – powerful commitment and emotional attachment to their ideas, new ventures, and the roles they play while launching and developing these new businesses (e.g. Cardon et al., 2009). Further, because entrepreneurs personally identify with their ventures and constantly face the unknown, they are inherently likely to feel strong affect and emotions – both negative and positive (Delgado García et al., 2015; Doern & Goss, 2013; Morris, Kuratko, Schindehutte, & Spivack, 2012).

Before we move forward and discuss the role and empirical evidence regarding affect and emotions in the entrepreneurship field in more depth, it is important to clarify some definitions. As explained by Baron (2015, p. 1) in the Wiley Encyclopedia of Management, *the term affect has generally been defined in a large body of research as referring to a very broad range of feeling states. Affect, therefore, encompasses both moods, which are often relatively long-lasting in nature but not focused on specific events or objects (e.g., cheerfulness and depression), and emotions (e.g., anger, sorrow, and joy), which are often shorter in duration but more specifically directed toward a particular object (e.g., a person, an event, or an object). (Frijda, 1993)*

Referring to entrepreneurship, scholars usually define this process as the recognition that there exists, or can be created, of business opportunities: the evaluation of the desirability and feasibility of an opportunity for the focal person or firm; and the exploitation (and perhaps reformulation) of an opportunity (McMullen & Shepherd, 2006; Shane & Venkataraman, 2000). As per Cardon et al. (2012), by opportunity this study refers to

[a situation] in which new goods, services, raw materials, markets and organizing methods can be introduced through the formation of new means, ends, or means-ends relationships to create value. (pp. 2–3).

Considering these definitions together, when entrepreneurs' affect and emotions are investigated, the literature usually refers to

the affect, emotions, moods, and/or feelings – of individuals or a collective – that are antecedent to, concurrent with, and/or a consequence of the entrepreneurial process, meaning the recognition/ creation, evaluation, reformulation, and/or the exploitation of a possible opportunity. (Cardon et al., 2012, p. 3)

Keeping these definitions in mind, in the following paragraphs the main literature about the role of affect in entrepreneurship will be discussed.

1.2 AFFECT AND ENTREPRENEURSHIP: LITERATURE REVIEW

A recent review of the literature entitled *How Affect Relates to Entrepreneurship: A Systematic Review of the Literature and Research Agenda* (2015) by Juan Bautista Delgado García, Esther De Quevedo Puente, and Virginia Blanco Mazagatos offers an interesting categorisation of entrepreneurship research on affect. The authors explain that the extant literature in this area could be classified following four main criteria: the level of analysis, the antecedents and consequences of affect, the consequences of affect for the entrepreneurial process, and the facets of affect analysed (Delgado García et al., 2015).

1.2.1 The Level of Analysis

The first criterion is that it is important to consider is the level of analysis. Three levels of analysis can be considered: individual, interpersonal, and group (Delgado García et al., 2015). Most of the studies about the role of affect in entrepreneurship are focussed on the individual level of analysis, namely the entrepreneur. Of these, the most cited and important contributions by Baron and colleagues (Sassetti, Marzi, Cavaliere, & Ciappei, 2018) argue that affect plays an important role in the entrepreneurship process, from opportunity recognition to resource acquisition. In line with this, research has demonstrated that entrepreneurs' dispositional positive affect (DPA) is related to many beneficial outcomes, such as product innovation and sales growth (Baron & Tang, 2011), innovation, and creativity in general (Baron & Tang, 2011). At the same time, an increase in entrepreneurs' DPA is associated with damaging effects, for instance reduced task performance and higher impulsivity (Baron et al., 2012).

Few studies have examined the relationship between affect and entrepreneurship considering the interpersonal and group level. As explained by Delgado García et al. (2015), those research efforts which have considered the interpersonal level of analysis predominantly focus on the influence of positive affect displayed by entrepreneurs on the perceptions and decisions of other individuals, such as employees and investors (Breugst, Domurath, Patzelt, & Klaukien, 2012), or how negative affect displayed by the entrepreneur influences others' perceptions or decisions (Cardon, 2008). In this context, it is important to underline that:

> little is known on how affect displayed by other individuals influences the perceptions and decisions of the entrepreneur or on how affect displayed by an entrepreneur sways other members of an entrepreneurial team. This seeming lack of analysis is surprising, since affective influence between entrepreneurs and other individuals related to their ventures might be bidirectional – and because ventures are not always formed by a sole entrepreneur. (Delgado García et al., 2015, p. 199)

Finally, regarding the group level of analysis, it is evident that several studies have considered the effect of negative affect and business failure when a group entrepreneurial decision has to be made. In this regard, there is a need for a better understanding of how affect is distributed across social (different people and stakeholders) and organisational (entrepreneurial team, family business, and overall organisation) actors. This is particularly true in these times of complexity and change as entrepreneurs' decisions have a wider range of influences and are often the results of negotiation with different stakeholders (Randolph-Seng et al., 2015; Sassetti et al., 2018).

1.2.2 Affect as an Antecedent or Consequence of Cognition

Most of the literature about affect and entrepreneurship is discussed within the entrepreneurial cognition (EC) literature. EC represents the knowledge structures that entrepreneurs use to make assessments, judgements, or decisions involving opportunity evaluation, venture creation, and growth (Mitchell et al., 2002; Randolph-Seng et al., 2015). Indeed, 'Affect is a pervasive part of the way we see the world' (Forgas, 1995). Moreover, as pointed out by Simon after developing his theory on decision making, '[...], in order to have anything like a complete theory of human rationality, we have to understand what role emotion plays in it' (Simon, 1987).

For this reason, it is important to understand the link, in terms of antecedents and consequences, between affect and cognition. From Delgado and colleagues' review, we know that the majority of the literature has focussed on the consequences of affect with regard to cognition, such as opportunity recognition and evaluation. This emphasis is not surprising given that researchers have traditionally emphasised the effects of cognition on the entrepreneurial process as opposed to the antecedents of EC (Mitchell et al., 2007). On the contrary, few studies explore the cognitive antecedents which have an impact on affect. Most studies of antecedents have focussed on business failure and grief (e.g. Shepherd, 2003). As underline by Delgado García et al. (2015), the disproportionate theoretical and empirical focus on the cognitive consequences of affect calls for new research which analyses the antecedents of entrepreneurs' affect and the dynamics between antecedents and consequences.

1.2.3 The Consequences of Affect for the Entrepreneurial Process

For many years, entrepreneurship studies have been conducted within the context of economics: entrepreneurship has been considered as the heart of economic development and the unit of analysis for such studies has essentially been the individual (Sciascia & De Vita, 2004). The first definition of entrepreneur was given by Cantillon (1755) in his *Essai sur la Nature du Commerce en General*. What first appeared as a link between economic activity and the role of the entrepreneur was his inclination to risk and his ability to manage situations of uncertainty. According to Cantillon, in fact, the entrepreneur is a speculator in search for profit from arbitrage, from buying at a certain price and selling at an uncertain price. Furthermore, Say (1846) introduced the concept of entrepreneur in his *Traite D'économie Politique* in the early 1800s. In his representation of the economic system, Say identifies the entrepreneurial activity in the art of superintendence and administration.

In Britain, following the Industrial Revolution, Mill (1848) identified the role of the entrepreneur in a supervisory activity and specified the requisite qualities. Among these qualities the economist underlines 'superior knowledge' and 'habitual rectitude of perception and judgment'. Other British economists have contributed to the development of a theory of entrepreneurship: unlike other later neoclassical economists, Marshall, Pigou, and Edgeworth studied the entrepreneurial phenomenon (Sciascia & De Vita, 2004). Marshall (1930) defined the entrepreneurial function in providing innovations and consequently progress, writing that the entrepreneur (employer) is 'the mastermind of the whole'. An entrepreneur is responsible for decision-making about what kinds of job have to be done, how, and by whom. It is important to underline how already in Marshall's formulation not all businessmen can be considered entrepreneurs in the previous example. Marshall's entrepreneur is innovative in operative terms, meaning that he innovates for efficiency more than efficacy; thus, Schumpeter had the possibility to develop his ideas in a fuller sense.

Schumpeter and Nichol (1934) saw the entrepreneur as the major agent of economic development. The concept of economic development covers the following five cases: (a) the introduction of a new good or of a new quality of a good; (b) the introduction of a new method of production; (c) the opening of a new market; (d) the conquest of a new source of supply of raw materials or half-manufactured goods; and (e) the carrying out of the new organisation of any industry. In his work, Schumpeter conceives the market as a system in equilibrium and entrepreneurship as the process of disrupting such equilibrium, a way of moving the market away from it. In order to understand Schumpeter's contribution to the research in the field it is important to underline that this kind of innovation comes from resources that already exist in the market and are already under the control of the entrepreneur. In this sense, innovation is not the consequence of an invention; rather, invention operates as an exogenous factor with regard to the economic dynamics. Of course, inventions could change the perceived value of some resources, but this can happen only after their implementation in the ordinary activity of the firms. While entrepreneurs may be inventors, the birth of an innovation itself does not require invention.

In contrast, Kirzner (1979), an Austrian economist, suggests that entrepreneurship is the consequence of innovations designed to exploit the opportunities afforded by economic disequilibrium. He therefore turns the Schumpeterian view upside down, depicting the entrepreneur as an equilibrator agent taking advantage of disequilibrium.

With these historical premises in mind, we should affirm that entrepreneurship is built around opportunities (McMullen & Shepherd, 2003; Shane & Venkataraman, 2000) that have to be recognised, evaluated, and managed. Accordingly, Delgado García et al. (2015) explain that most of the studies about the role of affect in entrepreneurship have considered the intermediate stages of entrepreneurial process, namely opportunity exploitation, venture management, and success. Most of these studies have considered positive affect; however, less is known about the role of negative affect. Specifically, we know that positive affect increases opportunity recognition, but researchers have also suggested that this beneficial effect has a limit (Baron, 2008; Cardon et al., 2009; Foo, Murnieks, & Chan, 2014). It is not clear whether the influence of positive affect on opportunity recognition increases at a lower rate as positive affect increases or whether there is a discrete threshold beyond which very high levels of positive affect may reduce opportunity recognition. Regarding the opportunity evaluation, the researchers (Baron, 2007, 2008; Baron et al., 2012) explain that positive affect can be useful in evaluating opportunities; however, at the same time if there is an exaggeration of positive disposition, it could become a bias and lead to an overestimation of some information and situations that could subvert the opportunity evaluation success.

Considering the exploitation phase, researchers have asserted that it is important both to understand the decision to exploit and also to consider how to collect financial, human, and material resources (Clarke, 2011). In this context, studies have focussed on understanding the interpersonal effects of affect, particularly positive affect (e.g. Breugst et al., 2012) in engaging potential resource providers. Specifically, Brundin, Wigren, Isaacs, Friedrich, and Visser (2008) and Clarke (2011) have outlined how entrepreneurs' affective displays influence employees' willingness to act entrepreneurially and signal to resource providers that their venture is feasible and legitimate. Some other studies have focussed on the perception of entrepreneurial passion by employee and investors (Breugst et al., 2012; Chen, Yao, & Kotha, 2009), concluding that that entrepreneurial passion perceived by investors positively influences the investors' evaluations of technologies.

Finally, examining the management and the success of the venture, studies have demonstrated that affect is related to innovation (Baron & Tang, 2011;

Baron et al. 2011; Morris et al., 2012), level of effort (Foo, Uy, & Baron, 2009), personal initiative and persistence (Cardon & Kirk, 2015; Hahn, Frese, Binnewies, & Schmitt, 2012), propensity to continue investments in an under-performing project (Brundin & Gustafsson, 2013), and the types of goals set (Delgado-García, Rodríguez-Escudero, & Martín-Cruz, 2012). It is also evident that affect has an influence on different measures of venture performance, including growth (Baum & Locke, 2004; Cardon et al., 2009), business income (Ho & Pollack, 2014), and satisfaction (Delgado-García et al., 2012).

1.2.4 The Facets of Affect

In entrepreneurship literature, when the role of affect and emotions is discussed, one of the main criteria that has to be considered is the facets of affect, specifically their valence, arousal, and cognitive appraisal tendency (Delgado García et al., 2015). The consideration of these three different aspects originates from psychological theory, which has considered the role of affect and emotions in judgement and decision-making (Clore, Schwarz, & Conway, 1994; Forgas, 1995; Schwarz & Clore, 1996; Zajonc, 1998).

One of the most important theories in this field is the affect infusion model (Forgas, 1995). According to this model, people rely on their present feelings in a heuristic fashion to make complex judgements, as long as the experienced feelings are perceived as relevant to the object of judgement (Clore, 1992). Most of the studies which adopted this theoretical perspective-based assumptions on the valence of the affect: positive or negative (Forgas, 1995). This means that positive and negative affect are experimentally induced or observed naturalistically, and these general feeling states are expected to lead to more positive or negative judgements, respectively (Lerner & Keltner, 2000). The valence approach has typically been described along two dimensions – positive and negative affect (Fillenbaum & Rapoport, 1970). Positive affect includes emotions such as joy and optimism, whereas negative affect includes emotions such as anger, depression, fear, and frustration.

Together with the valance of affect the affect infusion model usually also considers the arousal of the affect (Forgas, 1995), that is, the feeling state's degree of intensity. An individual's level of arousal may range from quiet to aroused.

The study of the influence of affect on judgements is also central to Lerner and colleagues' Appraisal Tendency Framework (ATF) (Lerner & Keltner, 2000; Lerner, Valdesolo, et al., 2015). Lerner and Keltner (2000) note that the existing research has predominantly taken a valence-based approach, focussing exclusively on positive versus negative feeling states in the form of undifferentiated positive or negative affect. Extending the feelings-as-information approach to specific emotions, the ATF argues that appraisal tendencies are goal-directed processes through which emotions influence judgements and decisions until the emotion-eliciting problem is resolved (Lerner & Keltner, 2000; Lerner, Li, Valdesolo, & Kassam, 2015). In particular, it asserts that emotions of the same valence (such as fear and anger) can exert contrasting influences on judgements and decisions, whereas emotions of the opposite valence (such as anger and happiness) can exert similar influences (Lerner, Li, et al., 2015).

The results of the literature review by Delgado García et al. (2015) explain that most of the studies about the role of affect in entrepreneurship mainly consider the valence of affect, with less attention paid to its arousal or cognitive appraisal tendency. In general, most of the research to date has focussed on positive affect, with the exception of research on business failure and grief (e.g. Shepherd, 2003). This disproportion could be due to the image of the entrepreneur as an optimistic and passionate individual (Cardon et al., 2009; Hmieleski & Baron, 2009) or to the potential beneficial effects of positive affect (Baron, 2008).

Due to the importance of investigating the valence of affect, both positive and negative, in the following paragraphs particular attention will be paid to understanding the results of those studies and their role within the entrepreneurship literature.

1.3 POSITIVE AFFECT AND ENTREPRENEURSHIP

Most of the research in the literature about the relationship between affect and entrepreneurship has focussed on positive affect (Delgado García et al., 2015). One of the main contributors in this field of research is Robert Baron. In 2011, Baron and Tang wrote an article entitled *The Role of Entrepreneurs in Firm-level Innovation: Joint Effects of Positive Affect, Creativity, and Environmental Dynamism*. This contribution investigates the relationships between two individual-level variables, namely entrepreneurs' positive affect and creativity and firm-level innovation. The findings of this research demonstrate that positive affect is related to entrepreneurial innovation. However, rather than being direct in nature, this effect is mediated. Specifically, creativity was found to mediate the relationship between entrepreneurs' positive affect and firm-level innovation.

In another study by Baron et al. (2012) entitled *Entrepreneurs' Dispositional Positive Affect: The Potential Benefits – and Potential Costs – of Being*

'*Up*', the authors developed and tested a theoretical model which considered the effect of DPA on individual-level processes, such as decision-making, identification and evaluation of opportunities, and the development and implementation of product innovations. The DPA is defined as the stable tendency to experience positive moods and emotions across many situations and over time. The authors started from the premise that across a large body of research conducted in several different fields (e.g. social and cognitive psychology, human resource management, and organisational behaviour) positive affect has been found to be associated with a wide range of benefits (Ashby & Isen, 1999; Weiss & Cropanzano, 1996). Consequently, Baron et al. (2012) have demonstrated that high levels of DPA can have detrimental effects on basic aspects of cognition, perception, motivation, and self-regulation. These effects, in turn, may reduce entrepreneurs' ability to perform key individual tasks.

In the same vein, during their research entitled *The Role of Affect in the Creation and Intentional Pursuit of Entrepreneurial Ideas* by Hayton and Cholakova (2012) developed a framework which suggests that regardless of disposition, positive affective states (moods and emotions) will exert a positive influence on the perception of entrepreneurial ideas. Their findings also include potential reasons for the apparently higher than average levels of positive dispositional affect among entrepreneurs (e.g. Hmieleski & Baron, 2009). Indeed, their theoretical development and the hypotheses testing show that entrepreneurs with a positive dispositional affect will be more likely to experience entrepreneurial ideas in comparison with those with negative dispositional affect. At any given time, an individual with higher levels of positive dispositional affect will be more likely to be in a positive affective state. Therefore, exposure to information, or the need to recall or combine information, will be more likely in a positive dispositional state. The disposition also increases the probability that at any point in the iterative cycle of idea development, the individual will benefit from the influence of positive affect.

More recently, a meta-analysis by Fodor and Pintea (2017) – '"Emotional side" of Entrepreneurship: A meta-analysis of the relation between positive and negative affect and entrepreneurial performance' – confirmed the previously identified significant and reliable relationship between positive affect and entrepreneurial performance. Specifically, this meta-analysis established that positive affect has a positive impact on certain dimensions of performance such as innovation, sales, venture growth, and goal attainment. As the authors affirmed:

> In short, PA is considered to activate the Behavioral Approach System (BAS), an underlying neuropsychological system that triggers

appetitive, reward seeking behaviors, which are aligned to the specifics of entrepreneurial tasks and conducive for performance.

Another recent contribution was written by Jia and Zhang (2018) and it is entitled *The Impact of Positive Affect on Entrepreneurial Motivational Outcomes – A Self-regulatory Perspective.* In this study, the authors investigated whether and to what extent positive affect influences three major motivational outcomes of work motivation (Locke & Latham, 1990) within the entrepreneurship area: direction, intensity, and persistence of entrepreneurial engagement after the initial entry into entrepreneurship. The results show that the level of positive affect significantly increases the likelihood that entrepreneurs are motivated by intrinsic orientation rather than extrinsic orientation, and significantly increases entrepreneurial persistence over a certain amount of time. Moreover, entrepreneurs are more likely to engage in entrepreneurship with an intrinsic motivation in situations of lower environmental uncertainty, whereas the impact of positive affect on entrepreneurial persistence is greater within a more uncertain and dynamic environment. The study underlines that the authors did not find evidence for a relationship between positive affect and entrepreneurial effort.

Finally, the contribution by Bernoster, Mukerjee, and Thurik (2020) entitled *The Role of Affect in Entrepreneurial Orientation* indicates that positive affect is positively associated with entrepreneurial orientation. Specifically, the authors specify that positive feelings and emotions are associated with acting in a more entrepreneurial manner in terms of innovativeness, proactiveness, and risk taking, although for small business owners positive feelings and emotions are primarily associated with innovativeness. The positive association between positive affect and innovativeness is consistent with earlier findings (Baron & Tang, 2011). A further consideration in this study is the role of affect in entrepreneurial success, with the authors highlighting a positive association between positive affect and entrepreneurial success.

1.4 NEGATIVE AFFECT AND ENTREPRENEURSHIP

Like positive affect, negative affect may have a positive function in entrepreneurship. In this field of research one of the main contributors is Maw-Der Foo et al. (2009, 2011). In a paper entitled *How Do Feelings Influence Effort? An Empirical Study of Entrepreneurs' Affect and Venture Effort,* based on control theory (Carver & Scheier, 1990), Foo et al. (2009) argue that negative affect functions as an indicator that progress towards the goal is inadequate and slower than expected. This should prompt entrepreneurs to invest more effort into urgent tasks. The authors' diary study provides support for this positive effect of negative affect. Furthermore, Foo (2011), in a study entitled *Emotions and Entrepreneurial Opportunity Evaluation*, also highlights that negative affect in the form of anger may have positive effects with regard to opportunity evaluation. Anger is associated with appraisal tendencies of high confidence and control, thus leading to lower risk perceptions and more positive opportunity evaluations (Foo, 2011).

In contrast, the contribution by Fodor and Pintea (2017) takes in consideration the effect of negative affect on entrepreneurial performance; contrary to pre-existing expectations they demonstrate that, overall, negative affect has no significant (negative) implications for entrepreneurial performance. As specified in the study,

> *this is surprising, since scholars have traditionally argued toward a more significant effect of negative affect on entrepreneurial processes. One argument concerned the increased frequency and intensity of negative affective experiences encountered during the entrepreneurial process (Doern & Goss, 2014; Markman et al., 2002). The other one claimed that negative affect has a higher influence on several psychological processes, as compared to positive affect. However, this non-significant should be approached with prudence due to the low number of studies that included measures for the negative affect and entrepreneurial performance relation. (Fodor & Pintea, 2017, p. 12)*

A more recent contribution by Stroe, Sirén, Shepherd, and Wincent (2020), *The Dualistic Regulatory Effect of Passion on the Relationship Between Fear of Failure and Negative Affect: Insights from Facial Expression Analysis*, originates with the premise that despite negative affect's important detrimental impact on the thinking, behaviour, and interactions of entrepreneurs (Baron, 2008; Foo, 2011; Grichnik, Smeja, & Welpe, 2010) as well as on venture success and survival (Baron, 2008; Hayton & Cholakova, 2012), there is very little research on the antecedents of negative affect in entrepreneurship. The few studies that have explored the antecedents of negative affect in entrepreneurship have focussed on business failure as an antecedent of the negative affective experience of grief (Shepherd, 2003). The theoretical and empirical focus on the consequences of negative affect in entrepreneurship calls for new research to analyse the antecedents of entrepreneurs' negative affect beyond business failure and explain how entrepreneurial tasks might influence the development of negative affective states. The contribution by Stroe et al. (2020) aims to fill this gap in the literature by responding to calls for research on the antecedents of negative affect in entrepreneurship (Cardon et al., 2012;

Delgado García et al., 2015); the study investigates how early-stage entrepreneurs experience negative affect during events typical of their profession as a result of fear of failure and how entrepreneurs' passion moderates this relationship. Their results indicate that entrepreneurs high in fear of failure experience more negative affect and that passion moderates this relationship.

While both studies show that harmonious passion reduces the influence of fear of failure on negative affect, the results of the two studies differ in terms of obsessive passion's moderating role in the relationship between entrepreneurs' fear of failure and their experience of negative affect while engaged in an entrepreneurial activity.

Finally, as explained in the previous paragraph, the contribution by Bernoster et al. (2020) with regard to affect (both positive and negative) and entrepreneurial orientation indicates a positive association between positive affect and entrepreneurial orientation. Conversely, negative affect is negatively associated with entrepreneurial orientation. The authors considered two different samples – sole proprietors and small business owners – and specified that although there was a negative association between negative affect and individual entrepreneurial orientation for sole proprietors, there was no significant negative association between negative affect and firm entrepreneurial orientation in small business owners. Consequently, these findings suggest that for sole proprietors having negative feelings and emotions is associated with a less entrepreneurial strategic posture (particularly with respect to innovativeness and risk taking), whereas negative feelings and emotions experienced by small business owners do not impact their firm's strategic posture. Hence, unlike sole proprietors, the affective characteristics of the small business owner alone do not impact firm entrepreneurial orientation. A possible explanation is that firms, as opposed to sole proprietors, are confronted with task conflicts and relationship conflicts, both of which impact negative affect (Breugst & Shepherd, 2017). These conflicts can also impact the strategic posture of the firm.

2

UNVEILING THE CONNECTION BETWEEN EMOTIONAL INTELLIGENCE AND ENTREPRENEURSHIP

2.1 DEFINING EMOTIONAL INTELLIGENCE

Salovey and Mayer (1990, 1997) were the first to propose the concept of emotional intelligence (EI). They defined it as emotional knowledge, the ability to perceive, evaluate and express emotions accurately and adaptively, the ability to generate and/or utilise sentiments with the aim to facilitate cognitive activity and adaptive behaviour, and, finally, the ability to manage emotions within oneself as well as in relation to others. Subsequently, Goleman made EI popular in his famous works of 1995 by defining its role in achieving success in life as essential and even superior to traditional intelligence.

Despite the fact that the concept of EI in no way lacks innovative perspectives, it represents the development and research into a series of theoretical proposals which had already been formulated in the study of intelligence. In fact, among the classical theories on intelligence some mainly focussed on the basic cognitive abilities (Binet, 1905; Spearman, 1923), whereas others suggested increasing the number of factors influencing the construct of intelligence (Cattell, 1971; Thurstone, 1938), also drawing attention to the context of the individual. In this context a paradigmatic example is Sternberg's triarchic theory (1984), which suggests that intelligence is the result of abstract-logic processes (compositional intelligence); however, it is also the ability to adapt to the environment (contextual intelligence) and to take on new tasks and automate known ones (empirical intelligence). Other theories, anticipating the main themes of the concept of EI, highlighted the contribution of motivational and emotional-affective factors in defining intelligence. Although in the past some research efforts have considered thoughts and emotions as contrasting, even to the extent of considering the latter as an obstacle to rational thinking (Schaffer, Gilmer, & Schoen, 1940; Woodworth, 1940; Young, 1936), as early as Thorndike (1920) there is a reference to the concept of 'Social Intelligence' intended as the ability to understand and manage emotions. Moreover, as Kaufman and Kaufman (2001) observed, even Wechsler (1950) had anticipated the importance of emotional factors; he defined these as 'non-intellectual' or 'conative' (tied to the voluntary or intentional sphere), as facilitators or inhibitors of the intellectual processes. Nonetheless, with Gardner (2000) emotions gained the status of actual expressions of intelligence for the first time; in his theory of multiple intelligences, he places linguistic, logical-mathematical, physical-kinetic, spatial, and musical intelligence side by side, in addition to the concepts of 'intrapersonal' and 'interpersonal' intelligence. He considered the former as the ability to have access to your own feelings, represent them and use them as tools or guidelines to understand your behaviour, while the latter indicates the capacity to understand other people's feelings and act accordingly. Therefore, in Gardner's theory, we can trace the theoretical origins of the later definition of EI given by Salovey and Mayer (1990), who highlight the need to consider the crucial role of emotions in the ongoing relationship between individuality (in the cognitive, conative, and affective sense) and the socio-relational context in question. The authors consider emotions as systematic answers that have passed through several psychological subsystems; therefore, they consider elaborating and using meaningful emotional information as an integral part of intelligent behaviour (Salovey & Mayer, 1990).

2.2 EMOTIONAL INTELLIGENCE: A COMPARISON OF THEORETICAL MODELS

As mentioned above, the first theoretical model of EI is provided by two American psychologists, Peter Salovey and John D. Mayer, who published two articles in 1990. The first of these, *Imagination, Cognition and Personality* (Salovey & Mayer, 1990), was introductive and the other, *Journal of Personality Assessment*, was experimental, presenting preliminary demonstrations of the possibility of measuring EI (Mayer, DiPaolo, & Salovey, 1990). The authors define EI as the ability to understand and monitor feelings (both in oneself and others) and to use these feelings as a source of information for thought and action, divided into three components: evaluation and expression, adjustment, and use of emotions. Over time, the authors would review and modify this conceptualisation (Mayer & Salovey, 1997) and redefine it

(Mayer, Caruso, & Salovey, 1999; Mayer, Salovey, & Caruso, 2004; Salovey, Bedell, Detweiler, & Mayer, 1999). In the current model, EI is defined by the authors as a set of cognitive abilities to elaborate emotional-affective information regarding both the personal and interpersonal spheres. These abilities are divided into four main branches which are ordered hierarchically: (1) accurately perceive, evaluate, and express emotions; (2) generate and/or use emotions to facilitate thought; (3) understand emotions, their causal relations, their transformations, and the combination of emotional states; and (4) regulate and manage emotions to promote emotional and intellectual growth (Mayer & Salovey, 1997).

Possessing the higher-level abilities is considered essential in order to develop lower-level abilities (MacCann, Roberts, Matthews, & Zeidner, 2004; Mayer & Salovey, 1997). Additionally, the first two branches (perception and use of emotions) are considered 'experiential components', whereas the last two branches are considered 'strategic components' of EI (Mayer, Salovey, & Caruso, 2002). From this perspective, EI is understood as a genuine cognitive ability or a potential that interacts synergistically with the basic cognitive functions possessed by subjects and is not significantly influenced by cultural differences.

In the other EI models described below, the terms emotional ability and emotional skill are often used interchangeably. It is widely accepted that the term skill refers to possessing the necessary requirements to adequately complete a particular task. These requirements correspond to the possession of abilities, skills, knowledge, and behavioural capacity. However, the difference between ability and skill is the subject of ongoing debate in literature (Hoffmann, 1999) and their use, along with the definitions that emerge, are often contrasting or overlapping. This confusion is also present in EI models as the authors often do not always explain their reasons for using one term instead of the other and the subtle differences in meaning in other languages make the issue even more complex.

In his EI models, Goleman (1995) takes ownership of Boyatzis (1982) definition of emotional skill, described as the ability to recognise, understand, and use emotional information, related to oneself and others, leading to or producing an efficient or above-average performance. This definition has assumed a very peculiar connotation over time, in particular because of the close connection between EI and the workplace, as we can see from several works by Goleman and his collaborators (Boyatzis, Goleman, & Rhee, 2000; Goleman, Boyatzis, & McKee, 2002) and from the birth in 1996 of the Consortium for Research on Emotional Intelligence in Organisations; this body is still an important reference for research and development of EI theories in organisations used by individuals and companies alike. The current version of the model by Goleman (Boyatzis et al., 2000) identifies a set of specific skills divided into four domains: self-awareness, which refers to awareness of one's own emotions and use of these when making decisions; social awareness, which refers to empathy and understanding of social relations; self-management, which refers to control over one's emotions and ability to adapt to different situations; and relationship-management and management of social relations.

The most controversial definition of EI is the one suggested by Reuven Bar-On (1997), as the meaning of the terms used by the author are not particularly clear. He describes EI as a combination of non-cognitive abilities, skills, and learnt abilities that influence the skills of individuals in the moment of efficiently dealing with needs and pressures from the surrounding environment (Bar-On, 1997). Bar-On and Parker (2000) group these skills (or abilities?) into five different dimensions, which also include aspects of personality such as intrapersonal (self-awareness, emotional self-awareness, assertiveness, independence, and self-realisation), interpersonal (empathy, social responsibility, and interpersonal relations), stress management (stress tolerance and impulse management), adaptability (change management, adaptability, solving personal, and interpersonal problems), and general mood (optimism and happiness). Moreover, Bar-On defines these final characteristics, along with some others (self-realisation, independence, and social responsibility), as facilitators of emotional behaviour and social intelligence rather than actual components of EI (Bar-On, 2004); thus, his theory becomes yet more complex and somewhat contradictory (MacCann et al., 2004). The prevailing question that remains is whether it is correct to label the psychological dimension described by Bar-On's model with the term emotional 'intelligence' or rather as a group of personal characteristics linked to emotions. It is clear that, given their profound differences, trying to navigate the various EI models is not easy; however, an efficient way to organise them proposed by Mayer, Salovey, and Caruso (2000) involves distinguishing between mixed models and ability models. All the models that consider EI as a combination of behavioural tendencies, motivational and affective variables, considered relatively stable and not necessarily retraceable to intelligence, fall under the former category, as is the case with Bar-On (1997) or Goleman (1995). On the other hand, the theoretical frame outlined by Mayer and Salovey (1997), in which only variables of cognitive and mental ability are considered components of EI and all other dimensions relating to differences between individuals are dismissed as they do not meet the classic predefined criteria of intelligence, falls under the second category (Mayer et al., 1999).

2.3 EMOTIONAL INTELLIGENCE AND SKILLS

Picking up some of the elements proposed by Goleman (1995) and integrating McClelland's (1951) previous contributions, Boyatzis places skills in a wide context and describes them as behavioural manifestations of emotional, social, and cognitive intelligence. Intelligence, to be considered as such, must have certain characteristics: it must be observable in behaviour, it must be connected to biological functions (particularly to the neural and endocrine functions), it must be linked to results achieved at work or in life, it must be distinguishable from other constructs of personality, and the measurement of the construct must answer to the validation criteria (Boyatzis, 2008).

Referring back to Goleman's definition (1998), emotional skills are considered to be 'learnt abilities based on EI which translate into improved working performance'. Skills are inserted into a personality theory in an integrated and holistic perspective. This theory allows us to connect different elements and to understand the relations between (Boyatzis & Ratti, 2009) neural circuits and endocrine processes, motivations and traits, the values and the profound philosophy that guides an individual, and the skills and groups of skills demonstrated by the subject.

This integration of the physiological, psychological, and behavioural levels allows us to acquire a more complete picture of human complexity. Within this perspective, in order to understand the impact skills have on performance, it is important to observe how often an individual adopts certain behaviours, that is, how often they demonstrate certain skills. What distinguishes superior performers is having a set of skills beyond a 'tipping point'. The tipping point for each skill depends on the organisational context; certain skills will have more or less impact in different work environments. The division of skills in clusters is also important; Boyatzis (2006) observed that when senior partners used a group of skills belonging to a cluster beyond the tipping point, profits increased significantly. Which skills were used beyond the tipping point was irrelevant, as long as they used skills belonging to different clusters. This could explain why particularly brilliant leaders may exhibit diverse styles. One of the advantages of this approach to the concept of intelligence is the possibility of development it offers: a mastery of human talent that can be developed even as an adult. Various training programmes have been introduced to increase the level of EI and improve the skills connected to it. These programmes have shown significant results not only in the workplace; for instance, we saw an increase in the foundation of new companies but we also witnessed a positive impact in terms of success in life, with beneficial consequences with regard to looking for work and satisfaction in general (Cherniss & Adler, 2000).

2.4 MEASURING EMOTIONAL INTELLIGENCE

Self-assessment tests can be considered as one of the first ways to measure EI and these have been used in many studies conducted by organisations to ana- lyse the effects of EI on work performance. Although they are still one of the most popular methods of evaluation, these tests are subject to criticism for the inaccuracies that can emerge from self-assessment, which is based on the per- ception of the subject that has regarding their own level of EI. Therefore, the results may not be reliable if the participants deliberately intend to mislead or create untruthful images of themselves to give a more favourable impression. Another significant issue when it comes to measuring EI relates to the difficulty in identifying a universal measurement of this construct as several empirical models exist. Some studies have produced different results with regard to the levels of EI depending on whether their measurement tool was based on one of the models produced by Goleman (1995) or Bar-On (1997) or on the perfor- mance measurements conceived by Mayer and Salovey (1997) (Muyia, 2009).

After analysing the tools in-depth, a decision was made to focus on the following aspects: MSCEIT, the Emotional Quotient Inventory (EQ-i), the Emotional Competence Inventory (ECI), and Emotional and the Social Com- petency Inventory (ESCI).

MSCEIT is the instrument obtained after updating MEIS, a scale devel- oped by Mayer, Salovey, and Caruso (1999). Essentially it is an ability test in which the candidate is asked to complete different tasks designed to evaluate the various dimensions of EI. The second version of this scale (V.2) allows us to measure the level of EI in the four branches of Mayer and Sal- ovey's (1997) ability model, providing an overall EI score which reflects the candidate's ability to deal with emotional information as well as four intermediate scores for the following dimensions: perception of emotions, integration and assimilation of emotions, knowledge of emotions, and man- agement of emotions. This tool contains 141 items, making it shorter and easier for candidates to complete compared to the original version. One of the principal limitations of this kind of test is still creating items that can be evaluated objectively. The score is calculated using the criteria of gen- eral consensus and that of experts. The former reflects the degree of agree- ment between the choices of the candidate and those of the standardisation group, while the latter reflects the degree of agreement between the choices of the candidate and the group of experts in the study of emotions. Some authors (e.g. Matthews et al., 2006) have expressed concerns regarding the procedure of assigning points based on expert consensus. Despite the criticism, vari- ous empirical studies have used this scale of measurement and examined the relationship between levels of EI and performance. Janovics and Christiansen

(2001), for instance, carried out a study using students who were working part-time, highlighting a positive correlation between their EI score and their supervisor's performance evaluation. Moreover, high levels of EI have been associated with more effective leadership (Kerr, Garvin, Heaton, & Boyle, 2006) and a stronger ability to create satisfying interpersonal relationships (Brackett, Mayer, & Warner, 2004; Lopes, Salovey, & Straus, 2003).

The second evaluation tool we analysed is the one developed by Bar-On (1997) – the EQ-i. This test has 133 items in the form of statements on behalf of the subject regarding their feelings, thoughts, and habitual behaviour. For each element, the candidate is required to express an opinion on a scale ranging from 1 to 5. The results of the test allow the researcher to obtain an overall score relative to emotional quotient (EQ) and intermediate points in the dimensions and sub-dimensions that constitute Bar-On's model. The studies that used this tool have highlighted positive connections between EQ levels and physical and psychological wellbeing (Slaski & Cartwright, 2003) as well as a favourable link with performance. For example, a study conducted by Langhorn (2004) on a sample of 100 managers revealed that the EQ-i scores of the participants allowed them to predict the annual increase in profits and customer satisfaction.

The last evaluation tool of EI analysed is the ECI, which is based on the mixed model theorised by Goleman (1998) and, therefore, takes a behavioural approach to EI. The tool was perfected by Boyatzis, Goleman and Rhee (1999) and consists of a 360° questionnaire which includes a self-assessment section and a section with opinions from external evaluators such as colleagues and supervisors. It was created with the intent to evaluate the emotional skills of individuals and the positive behaviour displayed by the subject. More specifically, it is based on the skills identified by Daniel Goleman in *Working with Emotional Intelligence* (1998), *Hay/McBer in Generic Competency Dictionary* (1996), and Richard Boyatzis in *Self-Assessment Questionnaire* (SAQ) (Wolff, 2005). The 2.0 version of this tool includes 18 skills divided into four clusters: self-awareness, self-management, social awareness, and relationship management.

Despite the value demonstrated by many studies on the measurement of EI using ECI, some criticism has emerged due to the lack of sufficient differences between some clusters. By value in psychological tests, we mean the degree of precision with which a questionnaire or test manages to successfully measure what it declares to measure. In order to meet more rigorous demands and identify a psychometric standard of a higher level, some refinements were made; these lead to Goleman, Boyatzis and McKee (2013) perfecting the model and developing the ESCI. This is also a multisource rater tool, which includes both self-evaluation and the opinions of external evaluators (Boyatzis, Gaskin, &

Wei, 2015). It is important to remember that with these sorts of tools, which are reliant on 360° evaluations, the opinions are expressed by people close to the subject. We have progressed from evaluation tools using behavioural sources, such as monitored simulations, to Behavioural Event Interview, analysed by experts specially trained to interpret behaviour, and finally to evaluations conducted by subjects, not purposely trained, who are asked to evaluate an individual and their behaviour (Boyatzis, 2007). To facilitate the evaluation process and ensure the reliability of the opinions in the ESCI version, the evaluators are provided with descriptions designed to guide them in understanding the underlying intent of certain behaviour. The new instrument for skills evaluation is comprised of four clusters (self-awareness, social awareness, self-management, and relationship management) and 12 skills, instead of 18, which are assessed using 68 items in the ESCI version.

2.5 EMOTIONAL INTELLIGENCE AND ENTREPRENEURSHIP: LITERATURE REVIEW

Having outlined the concept of EI in the previous section, now the focus is on understanding how EI has been investigated in the field of entrepreneurship. There is a general agreement that entrepreneurship refers to a set of activities or behaviours (Gartner, 1988; Kuratko, 2007; Shane & Venkataraman, 2000). Considering this view of entrepreneurship, the antecedents, behaviours, and consequences of entrepreneurship are a function of an individual's personality (Kuratko, 2007; McKenzie, Ugbah, & Smothers, 2007) and in this scenario EI may have a key role to play (Cardon et al., 2012).

Over time many studies have been published and the aim of this section is to summarise the main contributions regarding the relationship between EI and entrepreneurship. Specifically, the recent academic research in this field has been classified to understand the role of EI in the following areas: antecedents of entrepreneurship, such as entrepreneurial intention and orientation; entrepreneurial behaviour, for example, innovation; and finally the consequences of entrepreneurship, specifically venture performance.

2.5.1 Emotional Intelligence and Entrepreneurial Antecedents

The article entitled *Emotional Intelligence and Entrepreneurial Orientation. The Moderating Role of Organizational Climate and Employees' Creativity*, published by Mohammad Suleiman Awwad and Hanane Kada Ali (2012), examines entrepreneurs' EI within the context of entrepreneurial orientation.

Moreover, the researchers consider two related factors associated with entrepreneurial orientation: organisational climate (OC) and employees' creativity. The main contribution of this study is the fact that entrepreneurs' EI is an important personality predictor and antecedent of entrepreneurial orientation. Nonetheless, this link is indirect, mediated by OC and employees' creativity. At the same time, the researchers provide evidence that EI plays a critical role in creating a positive OC within small and medium enterprises (SMEs). On the other hand, this factor has no direct effect on employees' creativity whereas the OC can moderate this relationship; entrepreneurs with high EI are able to foster an OC in which their employees' creativity can flourish.

Roxana Andreea Mortana, Pilar Ripolla, Carla Carvalhob, and M. Consuelo Bernala (2014) wrote an article entitled *Effects of Emotional Intelligence on Entrepreneurial Intention and Self-Efficacy*. This study was based on the fact that despite the increasing interest in EI as a key factor for career success, to date little research had analysed the relationship between EI and individual differences in entrepreneurship, such as entrepreneurial intention (Ahmetoglu, Leutner, & Chamorro-Premuzic, 2011; Zampetaskis, Beldekos, & Moustakis, 2009). For this reason, the researchers proposed a study which analysed the relationships between the EI dimensions, namely appraisal and expression of emotions, regulation of emotions, and utilisation of emotions and entrepreneurial intention. Moreover, the authors postulated that this relationship would be mediated by entrepreneurial self-efficacy. The results show that EI plays an important role in the prediction of entrepreneurial processes, confirming the relationship between certain EI dimensions and entrepreneurial intention mediated by self-efficacy. The capacity to regulate and use emotions properly impacts the perception of self-efficacy that, in turn, can inspire youngsters to take entrepreneurial pathways. These results indicate that individuals with the capacity to regulate and use emotions effectively are more likely to believe they can be successful in entrepreneurial activities; therefore, they feel more effective and have more possibilities to engage in starting a new business. Thus, this study provides a small but contribution to support the concept that EI is an important element for being successful in creating a new business.

2.5.2 Emotional Intelligence and Entrepreneurial Behaviours

As explained by Zampetaskis, Beldekos, and Moustakis (2009, p. 167),

> *in a broad sense, entrepreneurial behavior captures all actions taken by an organization's members that relate to the discovery, evaluation and exploitation of entrepreneurial opportunities (Kuratko,*

Ireland, Covin, & Hornsby, 2005). In the literature, however, there is little agreement regarding the specific actions that constitute entrepreneurial behaviour within an organizational context. The various conceptualizations of entrepreneurial behaviour are often associated with discrete entrepreneurial events such as the creation of new organizations, new entry or new product development and innovation. (e.g. Covin & Slevin, 1991; Endres & Woods, 2006; Lumpkin & Dess, 1996)

Starting from this premise, Zampetaskis et al. (2009) wrote a paper entitled *"Day-to-Day" Entrepreneurship Within Organisations: The Role of Trait Emotional Intelligence and Perceived Organisational Support'*. Specifically, their work adopts Mair's (2005) conceptualisation of 'day to day' entrepreneurship, where individual entrepreneurial behaviour includes a spectrum of activities ranging from independent/autonomous to integrative/cooperative behaviour, aiming at an entrepreneurial way of getting things done. This chapter investigates the role of perceived organisational support (POS) and trait EI on individual entrepreneurial behaviour at lower levels within the organisational hierarchy. The study also examines the extent to which employee organisation tenure moderates the linkage between POS and entrepreneurial behaviour, demonstrating that employees who believe they have received high levels of support from the organisation will tend to reciprocate with positive attitudes and behaviours. Therefore, POS may be considered more suitable than the management support construct for the investigation of individual entrepreneurial behaviour at the lower hierarchical levels of the organisation. The second point relates to the fact that this study is the first to demonstrate that organisation tenure interacts with POS to influence individual entrepreneurial behaviour. Indeed, the research findings indicate that tenure moderates the relationship between POS and entrepreneurial behaviour such that the positive relationship between POS and entrepreneurial behaviour is stronger for employees with shorter tenure compared to those with longer tenure. This interaction effect is new to both the POS and entrepreneurship literature. Finally, their results show that employee trait EI has a significant relationship with entrepreneurial behaviour. This implies that employees with high trait EI are more aware of the factors contributing to their experience of positive and negative emotions. Accordingly, awareness of the factors that elicit certain emotions and understanding the effects of those emotions enable employees with high EI to take an appropriate actions influencing entrepreneurial behaviour.

One of the main issues investigated within the field of entrepreneurial behaviour is the innovation process (Endres & Woods, 2006; Lumpkin &

Dess, 1996). For this reason, it is not surprising that there is a specific interest in investigating the role of EI with regard to entrepreneurial innovation.

In a 2011 article entitled *EQ-nomics: Understanding the Relationship Between Individual Differences in Trait Emotional Intelligence and Entrepreneurship*, Ahmetoglu, Leutner, and Chamorro-Premuzic found that individuals high in EI tend to have higher affectivity, informing creative dispositions and thus facilitating innovation. Specifically, the authors connected EI to entrepreneurial behaviour and success, controlling for personality traits, demographic variables, and individual differences in entrepreneurial personality. More specifically, the study explores whether EI positively predicts entrepreneurial activity and achievement, and if Core Self-Evaluation (CSE) and Measure of Entrepreneurial Tendencies and Abilities, which are personality measures, have the potential to positively predict entrepreneurial activity. The results indicate that EI correlates significantly with most entrepreneurial outcomes under study, that is, entrepreneurial behaviour to generate income, corporate entrepreneurship, social entrepreneurship, entrepreneurial activity during school/college, and entrepreneurship through innovation. Thus, in this study the authors demonstrate that EI has an incremental validity in the prediction of some entrepreneurial activities beyond that of other personality and demographic variables. Further, in line with previous research, they suggest that emotionally intelligent individuals are more likely to engage in innovative entrepreneurial activities; they also tend to have higher affectivity, informing creative dispositions, and facilitating innovation, which are key aspects of entrepreneurship.

In the same vein, the paper entitled *Emotional Intelligence and Entrepreneurs' Innovativeness towards Entrepreneurial Success: A Preliminary Study* by Ngah and Salleh (2015) specifically focuses on the relationship between EI and innovation. The authors consider innovation as a key aspect of entrepreneurship. Entrepreneurs must be innovative as well as proactive and willing to take risks, while entrepreneurial orientation represents the policies and practices that provide a basis for entrepreneurial decisions and actions. Innovativeness is the predisposition to engage in creativity and experimentation through the introduction of new products/services as well as technological leadership via R&D in new processes. EI facilitates innovativeness and change within the organisation. The stressful and demanding environment requires strong mental strength in other to withstand the competition and remain sustainable over longer periods of time. For these reasons, this study aims to assess the relevance of two constructs: EI and entrepreneurs' innovativeness in entrepreneurial success.

The findings provide evidence that entrepreneurs need EI in order to innovate. Emotion has a significant influence over innovation, especially in understanding consumers' needs and wants. Regulation of the emotions of others has a strong impact on innovativeness and entrepreneurial success compared to other EI dimensions. The Ngah and Salleh (2015) study also suggests that there are no differences in gender in terms of EI and innovativeness for entrepreneurial success. Male entrepreneurs' perceptions of entrepreneurial success tend to be higher compared to their female counterparts. This is because male and female entrepreneurs tend to derive satisfaction from different sources; whereas male entrepreneurs place greater emphasis on status-based sources of business success, female entrepreneurs place greater emphasis on socio-emotional sources of business success such as building satisfying relationships with employees.

2.5.3 Emotional Intelligence and Entrepreneurial Consequences

One of the first contributions to the relationship between EI and entrepreneurship was a 2003 article by Cross and Travaglione entitled *The Untold Story: Is the Entrepreneur of the 21ˢᵗ Century Defined by Emotional Intelligence?* The authors conducted a qualitative study involving structured and in-depth interviews with five high profile Australian entrepreneurs. The research model based on an integration of two different models of EI: the EQ model by Mayer, Caruso, and Salovey (1999) and the EQ Workplace model by Goleman (1998). Therefore, they investigated the four components of EI proposed by Mayer et al. (1990), namely (1) perception, appraisal, and expression of emotion; (2) emotional facilitation of thinking; (3) understanding, analysing, and employing emotional knowledge; and (4) reflective regulation of emotions to further emotional and intellectual growth. Moreover, the authors also considered the EI personal competencies proposed by Goleman (1998): self-awareness, self-regulation, motivation, empathy, and social skills. Analysis of the results showed significantly high levels of overall EI among all respondents, as well as ighly satisfactory results for all the sub-scales of the two EQ models. Specifically, the main results of this study indicate that entrepreneurs have extremely high levels of appraisal and expression of emotion, as well as regulations and utilisation of emotion. With a greater ability to identify, understand, and manage the emotional responses of themselves and others, entrepreneurs will obtain a competitive advantage that sets their business performance apart from their competitors.

More recently, Ingram et al. (2019) published an article entitled *Emotional Intelligence and Venture Performance*. In this study, they respond to the call by Cardon et al. (2012) for an investigation into the role of EI in entrepreneurship, and to Foo et al. (2009) suggestion that EI might influence venture outcomes. Specifically, the authors assert that the emotional aware- ness and regulation inherent in EI will be consequential in addressing both the entrepreneur's problem-solving and decision-making challenges (intrap- ersonal abilities) and the social demands (interpersonal abilities) with inter- nal and external stakeholders. Consequently, they develop and test a model that addresses the direct effects of both the intrapersonal and interpersonal dimensions of EI on venture performance, as well as the indirect effects of these two aspects of EI on performance via interpersonal processes that entail team functioning in key tasks within the venture. The results demonstrate that interpersonal EI has a positive direct influence on venture performance; indeed, owners who are more skilled in appraising and managing others' emotions reported higher performance for their ventures. It is plausible that venture performance is enhanced because owners who are better versed in interpersonal emotions are more effective in terms of the social functioning demands of the venture, ultimately leading to better social network ties for resources and promotion of the venture. Importantly, this result extends the findings on the positive effect of EI on individual job performance to the level of the firm in entrepreneurship. The same cannot be said for intraper- sonal EI, which, contrary to expectations, did not exhibit a significant direct effect on performance. The self-management of emotions in intrapersonal EI does not appear to have an influence on the owner's individual actions in the venture (at least in a manner which is directly meaningful with regard to per- formance). Perhaps the significance of interpersonal EI, but not intrapersonal EI, is explained by the suggestion of Cherniss (2010) that EI, as the ability to perceive, understand, and manage emotion, might not be as strong a direct predictor of performance in comparison to specific social competencies. Here, interpersonal EI is more directly consistent with these social competencies, while the intrapersonal component of EI captures self-awareness and manage- ment of emotion. These results suggest there is value in examining the unique effects of the two types of EI on venture performance. They also indicate that both the interpersonal and intrapersonal dimensions of EI are indirectly asso- ciated with firm performance via interpersonal process effectiveness, which addresses tasks associated with business effectiveness.

3

THE EMOTIONAL SIDE OF ENTREPRENEURS' VENTURE PERFORMANCE: THEORETICAL FRAMEWORK AND RESEARCH DESIGN

3.1 THEORETICAL FRAMEWORK

In the previous chapters, the author aimed to collect and explain the main contributions regarding the relationship between affect, EI, and entrepreneurship. Based on this literature review, in the following paragraphs some hypotheses are presented and the related theoretical framework to be tested is explained. In the second part of the chapter, the focus is on explaining the research method adopted to test the theoretical framework. The data collection, the research setting, and the sample are also described.

Specifically, the aim of this research is to investigate the emotional side of venture performance; in order to do so, the hypotheses which compose the theoretical framework consider affect, positive and negative, and EI, explaining how these emotional components should be related to entrepreneurs' venture performance.

3.1.1 Positive Affect and Venture Performance

As explained in Chapter 1, most of the research in the literature about the relationship between affect and entrepreneurship has focussed on positive affect (Delgado García et al., 2015). The research demonstrated the impact of positive affect on innovation (Baron & Tang, 2011), cognition, perception and self-regulation (Baron et al., 2012), entrepreneurial ideas (Hayton &

Cholakova, 2012), entrepreneurial orientation (Bernoster et al., 2020), and motivation (Baron et al., 2012; Jia & Zhang, 2018).

As demonstrated within the research efforts noted above, in the field of entrepreneurship results support the benefits associated with experiencing positive affect (PA) for both individual and company performance (Fodor & Pintea, 2017). There is a general agreement that venture performance is a multidimensional construct (Venkatraman & Ramanujam, 1986), that performance measurement is a difficult task (Brush & Vanderwerf, 1992), and that choice of performance measures is a critical issue in research (Cooper, 1993). Inspired by the meta-analysis of Mayer-Haug, Read, Brinckmann, Dew, and Grichnik (2013) the venture performance concept can be considered as a combination of different performance effects (Mayer-Haug et al., 2013), for instance number of employees, sales, revenues and turnover, return on sales, net income and profit, liquidity, and overall financial measures (which are a combination of different financial measures).

In line with the aim of this research, the entrepreneurship literature has demonstrated that positive affect is significantly related to the statement of a broad and ambitious set of goals and satisfaction with business performance (Delgado-García et al., 2012). It enhances entrepreneurs' effort with regard to both present- and future-oriented entrepreneurial tasks (Foo et al., 2009), and stimulates cognitive flexibility and creativity (Baron & Tang, 2011) – important precursors of innovation as a measure of company performance. In addition, positive affective traits are associated with product innovation and increased sales rate up to an inflection point (Baron et al., 2011). Moreover, a meta-analysis by Fodor and Pintea (2017) confirms the significant and reliable relationship between positive affect and entrepreneurial performance, especially with regard to dimensions of performance such as innovation, sales, venture growth, and goal attainment. In line with these previous research efforts, this study postulates that positive affect has a significative and positive effect on venture performance.

H1. Positive affect is positively related with venture performance.

3.1.2 Negative Affect and Venture Performance

As explained in Chapter 1, like positive affect, negative affect may have a positive function in entrepreneurship. For example, Foo et al. (2009) have argued that negative affect functions as information that an individual's progress towards the goal is inadequate and slower than expected. This should prompt entrepreneurs to invest more efforts into tasks that are required on an immediate basis. The authors' diary study provides support for this positive effect of negative affect. Furthermore, Foo (2011) has shown that negative affect in the form of anger may have positive effects for opportunity evaluation. Anger is associated with appraisal tendencies of high confidence and control, thus leading to lower risk perceptions and more positive opportunity evaluations (Foo, 2011).

On the contrary, the contribution by Fodor and Pintea (2017) takes the effect of negative affect on entrepreneurial performance into consideration and demonstrates that, overall, negative affect has no significant implications with regard to entrepreneurial performance. Nevertheless, a positive relationship between negative affect and venture performance can be hypothesised. Indeed, as explained in Sassetti, Cavaliere, and Lombardi (2019), prior studies have led scholars to suggest that negative affect, facilitating systematic and analytic information processing (e.g. Forgas, 1995, 2000; Forgas & George, 2001; Schwarz, 2000) and applying a 'more detail-oriented, bottom-up, and vigilant processing styles' (Kuvaas & Kaufmann, 2004, p. 61), may lead to information processing that reduces or even eliminates common judgemental biases, as well as other cognitive mistakes in social thinking (e.g. Forgas, 2000). In a similar vein, scholars have found that negative moods help decision-makers follow a structured decision protocol when facing complex decisions (Elsbach & Barr, 1999); in so doing, they tend to reduce strategy bias in solving problems (Kaufmann & Vosburg, 1997). Thus, when negative emotions are felt, people tend to perceive the overall situation as unfavourable and engage in detailed and careful analysis to avoid mistakes in an attempt to improve the current affective state (Elsbach & Barr, 1999) and consequently improve venture performance. Considering the previous literature, this study postulates that negative affect has a positive effect on entrepreneurs' venture performance.

H2. Negative affect is positively related with venture performance.

3.1.3 Emotional Intelligence and Venture Performance

As explained in Chapter 2, Goleman (1998) described emotional skills as learnt abilities based on emotional intelligence which translate into improved working performance. Skills are inserted into a personality theory in an integrated and holistic perspective in which, in order to understand the impact skills have on performance, it is important to observe how often an individual adopts certain behaviours. In other words, how often do they demonstrate certain skills?

Boyatzis (2009) explains that research published over the last 30 years or so shows us that outstanding leaders, managers, advanced professionals, and people in key jobs, from sales to bank tellers, appear to require three clusters of behavioural habits as threshold abilities as well as three clusters of competencies which distinguish outstanding performance. The three clusters of competencies that differentiate outstanding performers from average ones are: (1) cognitive competencies, such as systems thinking and pattern recognition; (2) social intelligence competencies, including social awareness and relationship management competencies, such as empathy and teamwork; and (3) EI competencies, including self-awareness and self-management competencies, such as emotional self-awareness and emotional self-control. Competencies essentially amount to an approach to emotional, social, and cognitive intelligence.

Following this theoretical framework and due to this study's aim of investigating the effect of EI on venture performance, the focus of this research is to understand which EI competencies may have an effect on venture performance. As explained by Boyatzis (2009), EI competencies are divided into two clusters. The first, the self-awareness cluster, concerns knowing one's internal states, preferences, resources, and intuitions. This cluster contains one competency – emotional self-awareness – recognising one's emotions and their effects. On the other hand, the self-management cluster refers to managing one's internal states, impulses, and resources. This cluster, in turn, contains four competencies: emotional self-control, which refers to keeping disruptive emotions and impulses in check; adaptability, which refers to flexibility in handling change; achievement orientation, which involves striving to improve or meeting a standard of excellence; and positive outlook, which refers to seeing the positive aspects of things and the future.

In Chapter 2, explaining the relationship between EI and the consequences of entrepreneurship, the focus was primarily on venture performance. Interestingly, recent research by Ingram et al. (2019) has developed and tested a model that addresses the direct effects of both the intrapersonal and interpersonal dimensions of EI on venture performance and the indirect effects of these two aspects of EI on performance via interpersonal processes that entail team functioning in key tasks within the venture. The results showed that interpersonal EI has a positive direct influence on venture performance. Owners who are more skilled in appraising and managing others' emotions reported higher performance for their ventures. The same is not true of intrapersonal EI, which, contrary to expectations, did not exhibit a significant, direct effect on performance. The self-management of emotions in intrapersonal EI does not appear to have an influence on the owner's individual actions in the venture in a manner directly meaningful for performance. Nevertheless, to the best of our knowledge, there is no recent contribution which links the EI competencies as theorised by Boyatzis (2009) and entrepreneurs' venture performance, even though existing research supports this hypothesis (Cross & Travaglione, 2003). Specifically, analysing the main research in the field of entrepreneurship, the results indicate that entrepreneurs have extremely high levels of appraisal and expression of emotion, as well as regulation and utilisation of emotion. With a greater ability to identify, understand, and manage both their own emotional responses and those of others, entrepreneurs will obtain a competitive advantage that sets their business performance apart from their competitors (Cross & Travaglione, 2003).

For these reasons, in the present study, I postulate that the two clusters of EI, self-awareness and self-management (Boyatzis, 2009), and more specifically the competences which belong to them (emotional self-awareness, emotional self-control, adaptability, achievement orientation, and positive outlook), have a positive effect on entrepreneurs' venture performance.

Consequently, the following hypotheses are postulated:

H3. Emotional self-awareness has a positive effect on venture performance.

H4. Positive outlook has a positive effect on venture performance.

H5. Adaptability has a positive effect on venture performance.

H6. Achievement orientation has a positive effect on venture performance.

H7. Emotional self-control has a positive effect on venture performance.

The above hypotheses are presented in Fig. 1.

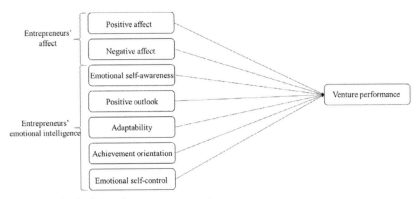

Source: Author's elaboration.

Fig. 1.   Theoretical Framework.

3.2 RESEARCH DESIGN

In order to test the theoretical framework discussed in the previous paragraph, a survey was constructed. In the field of entrepreneurship, a popular data source is survey data (Maula & Stam, 2020). Despite the known criticisms of the survey method (e.g. potential non-response bias, retrospective bias, common method bias, measurement error, and perceptual nature of data), one of the primary benefits is that surveys allow for the direct measurement of complex, latent constructs through multi-item scales. For many interesting entrepreneurship phenomena, the only way to obtain data is to ask people (Maula & Stam, 2020).

In order to provide as much rigour as possible (Maula & Stam, 2020), it is important to give a clear exposition of the survey data collection procedures and clarify how and why particular respondents were selected; what measures have been taken to minimise potential biases; and how the multi-item scales were constructed, adapted, and validated (Aguinis, Ramani, & Alabduljader, 2018).

Starting from these recommendations, in the following paragraphs the survey development and the data collection are presented and the sample and the procedure used to build the questionnaire are described.

3.2.1 The Survey Development and Data Collection

Data for this study was collected through a questionnaire administered to a sample of entrepreneurs of small and medium manufacturing firms in Tuscany, a region in Central Italy. Data were collected via a web-based questionnaire following the procedure suggested by Dillman, Smyth, and Christian (2014). As suggested by Fan and Yan (2010), it is important to keep in mind some factors which could affect the response rate and the efficacy of the web survey. The researchers explain that the response rate is significantly influenced by various factors, such as topics, length, ordering, and formatting of the web survey, long before respondents decide whether they will participate in the survey or not. In order to assess the quality of a web survey before its actual use, it is important to pilot the web survey with a small group of respondents in the real life situation and then invite content experts or methodology experts to review the pilot results. Moreover, factors such as sampling methods, contact delivery modes, invitation designs, informed consent methods, pre-notification and reminders, and incentive approaches have an influence over the response rate.

Following these suggestions, a report by the Regional Institute for Tuscany's Economic Programme (IRPET) has been analysed. A decision was made to focus on companies operating in the fashion and mechanical sectors, given their strategic relevance to the economic competitiveness of this area (IRPET, 2016). In order to identify the sample of companies to be observed, this study is reliant on the European Commission criteria defining SMEs: firm size, between 10 and 250 employees, and turnover, not higher than €50 million. The research population was composed of 3,734 SMEs listed at the Chamber of Commerce, 2,320 belonging to the fashion industry, and 1,414 to the mechanical industry. Following the literature (Elzahar, Hussainey, Mazzi, & Tsalavoutas, 2015), firms were randomly selected so that each industry, province area, and number of employees were represented by the same proportion as in the initial sample. In order to do so, all firms in each industry were ranked by their number of employees and province area; in addition, systematic sampling was used by retaining the first firm in every industry as a starting point, then the third, the fifth, and so on. Following this procedure, a total of 1,397 firms were identified. In order to administer the questionnaire, online company email addresses and telephone numbers were found via the internet; in case they were not available, the initial database was used to consider alternative companies and replace the firm in the final sample in accordance with the number of employees, industry, and province area. Moreover, some observations were excluded due to data unavailability. The final sample was composed of 1,261 SMEs' entrepreneurs, belonging to 755 fashion firms and 506 mechanical companies. As a consequence, 1,261 emails were sent to the entrepreneurs included in the sample. After the first invitation, sent in March 2017, 23 questionnaires were returned: 11 fully filled out and 12 partially filled out. Three rounds of reminders, one per week, were sent, thus generating 87 further complete responses. The final sample included a total of 98 entrepreneurs.

3.2.2 The Sample

Despite the fairly small sample size, it is similar to other studies which considered affective and cognitive variables (Baron & Tang, 2011; Baron et al., 2011). Moreover, consistent with Brigham, De Castro, and Shepherd (2007) work, the sample size may be considered small but the problem of external validity could be limited given the care in sample selection, the restricted population in which the results are generalised, and the fact that there was sufficient statistical power to detect the interactions of interest.

Regarding the sample characteristics, it is important to describe the characteristics of both the entrepreneurs and their venture. In terms of gender, among the 98 entrepreneurs, 78% are males and 22% are females (Fig. 2) and the average age is 52 years old. Because the majority of respondents are male, it is useful to consider this variable as a control variable during the discussion of the regression results in the following chapter.

Regarding the education level of entrepreneurs involved in this research, Fig. 3 shows that most of the entrepreneurs (53%) completed a High School course. Specifically, most of them attended technical high schools and have completed a specialised course of study that is related to specific vocational skills. A diploma of this type is proof that the individual has been exposed to information that

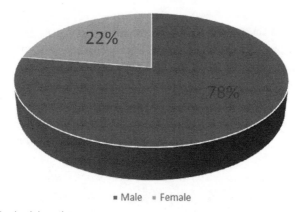

Source: Author's elaboration.

Fig. 2. Sample Description by Gender.

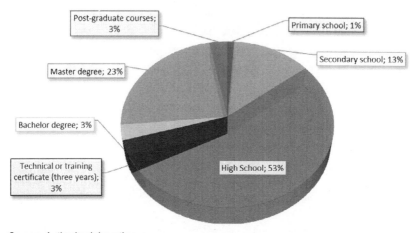

Source: Author's elaboration.

Fig. 3. Sample Description by Entrepreneurs' Education Level.

is vital to the performance of tasks associated with certain professions or jobs and has assimilated that information to the satisfaction of the institution that issued the certificates. Such education is typical in the area where the manufacturing sector is particularly developed; indeed, these industries need people that have developed knowledge, skills, competencies, and/or abilities required of a specific technical profession. This result is not surprising due to the sample involved in this research includes entrepreneurs who lead manufacturing ventures within the mechanical and fashion industries where specific technical skills are required. It is also interesting that 23% of the entrepreneurs involved in the research have a master's degree. This means that a new and old generations of entrepreneurs was involved in the research and, like gender, this variable will be valuable as a control variable.

From a firm point of view, 60.20% of the sample is fashion companies and 39.80% is mechanical ones. The average business tenure is 35 years. Fig. 4 shows the sample composition by the number of employees. The sample is primary composed of small firms (68%) which employ between 10 and 49 employees, while 17% are medium companies (50–249 employees). The final category, which includes microfirms, accounts for 14%. Although the sample procedure did not consider the microfirms, in the questionnaire we asked about the firm size and entrepreneurs had the possibility to indicate the category 'other'; those who chose this option indicated that they had less than 10 employees. This means that these firms lost some employees between the time when they listed at the Chamber of Commerce and the data collection period.

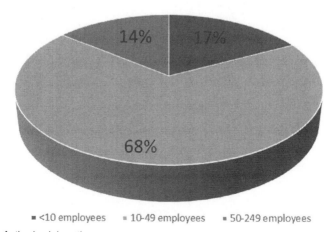

■ <10 employees   ■ 10-49 employees   ■ 50-249 employees

Source: Author's elaboration.

Fig. 4.   Sample Description by Number of Employees.

Similarly, the description of the firms involved in the research by their revenue (Fig. 5) shows that most of the firms have revenue of less than 10 million Euros (73%); indeed, only 16% of the firms in the sample have revenue higher than 10 million Euros and less than 50 million Euros. Finally, 10% indicated 'other' and most of them specified revenue higher than 50 million Euros.

Moreover, 68% of the firms that took part to the research are family businesses and the remaining 32% are not. In conclusion, the sample of this research is mostly composed of male entrepreneurs, baby boomers with a technical education. They mostly lead small family firms with revenue less than 10 million Euros.

3.2.3 The Questionnaire

Following the suggestions by Dillman et al. (2014) and Fan and Yan (2010), the information and data required was identified and then the type of question-naire to be built, its method of administration, the content of each question, their wording, and form of response were specified. Prior to its administration, the questionnaire was pilot tested with academics and practitioners working in the entrepreneurship field. Among the advantages of conducting pilot stud-ies are testing the adequacy of research instruments, assessing the feasibility of a survey, estimating variability in outcomes, collecting preliminary data, etc. Following the pilot test, the questionnaire was revised in order to produce a more valid data collection instrument. Consequently, some questions which had been previously included in the questionnaire were reformulated, others

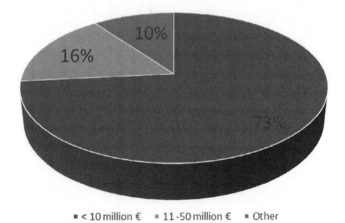

■ < 10 million €   ■ 11-50 million €   ■ Other

Source: Author's elaboration.

Fig. 5. Sample Description by Firms' Revenue.

were dropped, and new ones were added. The main objective was therefore to make sure the wording and the order of the questions were consistent with the purpose of the research. Hence, in line with Van Teijlingen and Hundley (2002), a pilot test can provide an advance warning about where the research could fail as well as whether the proposed research instruments are inappropriate.

Following the pilot test, the questionnaire was modified and various instrument and process design procedures were incorporated into the research design in order to minimise the common method bias, including guaranteeing anonymity (to address social desirability), use of industry-specific language (to reduce item ambiguity), and ensuring items in the questionnaire relating to the dependent variables were not located close to the independent variables (Ucbasaran, Westhead, & Wright, 2009). Although an independent source for the dependent variable would be desirable, self-report is unavoidable as affect and EI can only be measured by asking the entrepreneurs to talk about their feelings (Dewald & Bowen, 2010).

The variables included in the survey were operationalised through self-perception measures (Spector, 1994), primarily with 5-point Likert scales ranging from 1 (strongly disagree) to 5 (strongly agree). In the following section the details about the scales adopted are explained.

3.2.3.1 Measures

Before explaining the measures adopted in detail, Table 1 provides all relevant information regarding the number of items included in each measurement scale, the source from which the scales were taken, a brief description of each item, as well as the scale internal validity (Cronbach's α). Cronbach's α (or 'coefficient alpha'), developed by Lee Cronbach in 1951, measures reliability or internal consistency. 'Reliability' is how well a test measures what it should. Cronbach's α tests whether multiquestion Likert scale surveys are reliable. These questions measure latent variables, that is, hidden or unobservable variables such as a person's conscientiousness, neurosis, or openness. These are very difficult to measure in real life. Cronbach's α will determine whether the test designated is accurately measuring the variable of interest.

Table 1 shows good internal reliability of scales which ranges from 0.79 to 0.89. Moreover, all alpha coefficients clearly exceed the threshold level of 0.70 suggested by the literature (DeVellis, 2016; Nunnally, 1978; Robinson et al., 1991; Sekaran & Bougie, 2016).

Independent variables. Positive and negative affect. Affect was assessed using the 20 affect items from the Positive and Negative Affect Schedule (PANAS) (Watson, Clark, & Tellegen, 1988). On a 5-point rating scale (ranging from

Table 1.   Measurement Scales, Items, Source, and Cronbach's α for All Variables.

Variable	Items	Source	Item Sample	Measurement Scale	Cronbach's α
Positive affect	10	PANAS questionnaire by Watson et al. (1988)	'Interested, excited, enthusiastic'	1 = Not at all 5 = Very much	0.89
Negative affect	10	PANAS questionnaire by Watson et al. (1988)	'Distressed, upset, scared'	1 = Not at all 5 = Very much	0.89
Emotional self-awareness	4	Emotional and Social Competency Inventory (ESCI) by Boyatzis and Goleman (2007)	'I am able to describe how my own feelings affect my actions'	1 = Never 5 = Always	0.82
Positive outlook	5		'I see the positive in people, situations, and events more often than the negative'		0.88
Achievement orientation	4		'I initiate actions to improve my performance'		0.85
Self-control	6		'Acts appropriately even in emotionally charged situations'		0.79
Adaptability	6		'Adapts by smoothly juggling multiple demands'		0.81
Performance	5	Adapted by Wiklund and Shepherd (2003)	'Sales growth, revenue growth'	1 = Lower 3 = Higher	0.83

1= not at all to 5= very much), participants were asked how they generally experienced various feelings and emotions during strategic decision-making such as innovation and/or internationalisation decisions by referring to a list of 10 adjectives indicating positive affect (e.g. interested, excited, and enthusiastic) and 10 adjectives indicating negative affect (e.g. distressed, upset, and scared). The PANAS has been used to measure dispositional affect in previous studies by asking respondents to indicate how they feel on average (Baron & Tang, 2011; Baron et al., 2011; Barsky, Thoresen, Warren, & Kaplan, 2004). PANAS items were drawn from Zevon and Tellegen's (1982) mood checklist, in which items are grouped into various categories based on content. Items from the same content categories were permitted (Crawford & Henry, 2004). These content categories are presented in brackets after the items they represent for positive affect: attentive, interested, and alert (attentive); enthusiastic, excited, and inspired (excited); proud and determined (proud); and strong and active (strong). This is also done for negative affect: distressed and upset (distressed); hostile and irritable (angry); scared and afraid (fearful); ashamed and guilty (guilty); and nervous and jittery (jittery). The principal component analysis (PCA) and the consequent varimax rotation were performed, respectively, for all positive and negative affect categories in order to define the positive and negative affect variables.

In the current study, the measure produced a Cronbach's coefficient α for the positive affectivity scale of 0.89 and 0.89 for the negative affect. Both coefficients are higher than the reliability of the scale reported in previous studies (Baron et al., 2011; Baron & Tang, 2011; Barsky et al., 2004).

Independent variables – Emotional intelligence. As explained earlier in this chapter, following Boyatzis (2009), the EI competencies include self-awareness and self-management competencies. Specifically, the self-awareness cluster concerns knowing one's internal states, preferences, resources, and intuitions. This cluster contains one competency, namely emotional self-awareness. On the other hand, the self-management cluster refers to managing one's internal states, impulses and resources and contains four competencies: emotional self-control, adaptability, achievement orientation, and positive outlook. In order to investigate these EI competencies, the ESCI has been adopted based on the work of Boyatzis (2007) (Boyatzis & Sala, 2004). For each competency, the Cronbach's α was calculated. The results confirm the high reliability of the scales with all the values higher than the good threshold of 0.70 (Sekaran, 2000): emotional self-awareness (0.82), positive outlook (0.88), achievement orientation (0.85), self-control (0.79), and adaptability (0.81). The 5-point scales ranging from 'never' to 'always' were utilised.

Dependent variables – Venture performance. In order to assess the venture performance, the scale adopted was inspired by Wiklund and Shepherd (2003). Here, performance is considered to be multidimensional (Cameron, 1978) and that performance comparisons with competitors reveal important information (Birley & Westhead, 1990). Therefore, respondents were asked to compare the development of their own firm over the past three years relative to their two most important competitors for five different dimensions of performance: sales growth, revenue growth, growth in the number of employees, net profit margin, and adoption of new technology. This scale showed an excellent Cronbach's α (Sekaran, 2000) value of 0.83. We used 3-point scales ranging from 'lower' to 'higher'.

Control variables. Due to the sample analysis, both individual and firm control variables have been considered. Firm-level control variables included firm age at the year of data collection, industry (0 = Fashion; 1 = Mechanical), and size (0 = 10–49 employees/small firm; 1 = 50–250 employees/medium firm). Regarding the entrepreneurs, gender (0 = Male; 1 = female), age, and education level were also controlled.

4

DATA ANALYSIS AND MAIN FINDINGS

4.1 DATA ANALYSIS AND MAIN FINDINGS: OVERVIEW

This chapter aims to describe the empirical analysis conducted in order to test the theoretical framework. In the following sections, the descriptive statistics, considering the minimum and maximum value for each variable investigated and the related mean and standard deviation are described; moreover, the correlation matrix results are presented. Subsequently, CFA is performed. One of the main purposes of the CFA is the capacity to quantify the degree of model fit to the data (Thompson, 2004). The CFA model tests yield various statistics that quantify the degree of model fit. It is generally best practice to consult an array of fit statistics (Hu & Bender, 1999) in the hope that they will confirm each other (Thompson, 2004). This analysis is useful in order to demonstrate the reliability of the model tested. After the analysis of descriptive statistics, the results of regression analysis run using SPSS v.26 are reported. In order to test the hypotheses, seven different models have been designed and for each of them all the control variables (firm age and size; entrepreneurs' gender, age, and education level) have been entered. Finally, the main findings regarding the emotional side of venture performance are discussed.

4.2 DESCRIPTIVE STATISTICS

Descriptive statistics are shown in Table 2, where the minimum and maximum value for each variable investigated and the related mean and standard deviation are reported. The average values collected among participants in relation to the feeling of positive affect during the strategic decision-making process is higher (mean = 3.65) than negative affect (mean = 2.06). This suggests that

Table 2.   Descriptive Statistics of All Variables.

	N	Minimum	Maximum	Mean	SD
Positive affect	98	1.00	5.00	3.6593	0.70395
Negative affect	98	1.00	3.90	2.0615	0.63906
Self-awareness	98	2.00	5.00	3.8819	0.65015
Positive outlook	98	1.20	5.00	3.6989	0.79854
Adaptability	98	2.00	5.00	3.9048	0.60048
Achievement orientation	98	1.75	5.00	4.0824	0.76290
Self-control	98	2.00	5.00	3.5971	0.63928
Venture performance	98	1.00	3.00	2.3033	0.52861

entrepreneurs involved in the research have felt more positive emotions than negative ones during the decision to internationalise or innovate their firm.

Regarding the EI competences, the results indicate that the entrepreneurs perceived themselves as mostly able to strive to improve or meet a standard of excellence (achievement orientation; mean = 4.08) and to be adaptable and flexible in handling change (adaptability; mean = 3.90). Slightly lower values, but still high ones, have been recorded for emotional self-awareness, that is, the ability to recognise one's emotions and their effects (mean = 3.88); positive outlook, referring to the aptitude to see the positive aspects of things and the future (mean = 3.69); and the self-control competence, specifically the ability to keep disruptive emotions and impulses in check (mean = 3.59).

Finally, on average, the responses show that the sample of entrepreneurs expressed good value about their venture performance (mean = 2.3) based on a comparison between the development of their own firm over the past three years and that of their two most important competitors.

Table 3 shows the correlation matrix used to summarise data as an input into a more advanced analysis and as a diagnostic for advanced analyses. One way to quantify this relationship is to use the Pearson's correlation coefficient, which is a measure of the linear association between two variables. It has a value between −1 and 1: −1 indicates a perfectly negative linear correlation between two variables; 0 indicates no linear correlation between two variables; and 1 indicates a perfectly positive linear correlation between two variables. The further away the correlation coefficient is from 0, the stronger the relationship between the two variables becomes.

The analysis of the different variables considered in this research underlines that all the correlation values are less than 0.80, which means that there are no multicollinearity issues (Kennedy, 1985). Given this research's aim of investigating the emotional side of venture performance, that is,

Table 3.   Correlation Matrix for All Variables.

	1	2	3	4	5	6	7	8
1. Positive affect	1							
2. Negative affect	0.232*	1						
3. Self-awareness	0.388**	−0.103	1					
4. Positive outlook	0.524**	−0.072	0.325**	1				
5. Adaptability	0.597**	−0.166	0.486**	0.547**	1			
6. Achievement orientation	0.619**	0.046	0.426**	0.414**	0.618**	1		
7. Self-control	0.345**	−0.279**	0.270**	0.489**	0.433**	0.188	1	
8. Venture performance	0.214*	−0.059	0.065	0.245*	0.467**	0.245*	0.098	1

*Correlation is significant at the 0.05 level (two-tailed).
**Correlation is significant at the 0.01 level (two-tailed).

what the emotional antecedents of entrepreneurial performance are in terms of affect, both positive and negative, and EI competences. The correlation results between venture performance and the other variables considered in this study are described as follows:

- *Venture performance and adaptability*: the correlation between these two variables is positive (0.46) and quite strongly significant ($p < 0.01$).

- *Venture performance and achievement orientation*: the correlation between these two variables is positive (0.24) and significant ($p < 0.05$).

- *Venture performance and positive affect*: the correlation between these two variables is positive (0.21) and significant ($p < 0.05$).

- *Venture performance and negative affect*: the correlation between these two variables is negative (−0.05) and the coefficient is close to 0 – this means that no linear correlation can be considered and the correlation is not significant.

- *Venture performance and self-awareness*: the correlation between these two variables is positive (0.06) and the coefficient is close to 0 – this means that no linear correlation can be considered and the correlation is not significant.

- *Venture performance and self-control*: the correlation between these two variables is positive (0.09) and the coefficient is quite close to 0 – this means that no linear correlation can be considered and the correlation is not significant.

Considering these results, there is clearly a strong correlation relationship between venture performance and adaptability; in other words, the higher the adaptability the higher the job performance. Similarly, although to a lesser extent, there is a correlation between venture performance and achievement orientation and positive affect; specifically, the more achievement orientation and positive affect there is the better venture performance becomes.

It is important to remember that the correlation analysis does not give any suggestion about the cause–effect relationship between two variables. Rather, the correlation coefficient is a useful indicator of the nature of the relationship that binds two variables (how and how much they vary together, assuming that it is a linear relationship) but does not allow us to state if and to what extent one causes the other.

4.3 CONFIRMATORY FACTOR ANALYSIS FOR THE MODEL MEASUREMENT

CFA is a type of structural equation modelling that deals specifically with measurement models; that is, the relationships between observed measures or indicators (e.g. test items, test scores, and behavioural observation ratings) and latent variables or factors. The goal of latent variable measurement models (i.e. factor analysis) is to establish the number and nature of factors that account for the variation and covariation among a set of indicators. A factor is an unobservable variable that influences more than one observed measure and which accounts for the correlations among these observed measures. In other words, the observed measures are intercorrelated because they share a common cause (i.e. they are influenced by the same underlying construct); if the latent construct were to be removed, the intercorrelations among the observed measures would be 0. Thus, a measurement model such as CFA provides a more parsimonious understanding of the covariation among a set of indicators because the number of factors is less than the number of measured variables (Brown & Moore, 2012).

CFA can be used to confirm the factor structure identified in other exploratory analyses such as exploratory factor analysis. CFA requires pre-specification of all aspects of the model to be tested and is more theory-driven as opposed to data-driven, hence theory and/or prior research are crucial in specifying a CFA model to be tested (Harrington, 2009).

For this reason, in order to increase the reliability of the model tested in this research, after the deep theory construction and argumentation regarding the relationship between the variables considered, CFA has been identified as the most appropriate option.

One of the main purposes of CFA is the capacity to quantify the degree of model fit to the data (Thompson, 2004). The CFA model tests yield various statistics that quantify the degree of model fit. It is generally best practice to consult an array of fit statistics (Hu & Bender, 1999) in the hope that they will confirm each other (Thompson, 2004).

There are variety of goodness-of-fit statistics that provide a global descriptive summary of the ability of the model to reproduce the input covariance matrix. The classic goodness-of-fit index is X^2 (Brown & Moore, 2012). In addition to X^2 the most widely accepted global goodness-of-fit indices are absolute fit indices (Brown, 2006), which answer the question 'Is the residual (unexplained) variance appreciable?' (Chan, Lam, Chun, & So, 2006, p. 1012). The most common absolute fit index is the model chi-square, which tests whether the model fits into the population exactly.

Other absolute fit indices include the root mean square residual (RMR), which is the average discrepancy between the covariances in the input matrix and the covariances predicted by the model. Because the RMR is affected by the metric of the input variables, it can be difficult to interpret. The Standardised Root Mean Square Residual (SRMR) is based on the discrepancy between the correlations in the input matrix and the correlations predicted by the model; this model is standardised and therefore easier to interpret and, consequently, is generally preferred over the RMR (Brown, 2006).

Considered together, these indices provide a more conservative and reliable evaluation of the fit of the model. In one of the more comprehensive and widely cited evaluations of cut-off criteria, the findings of simulation studies conducted by Kline (2015) suggest the following guidelines for acceptable model fit: X^2 with a non-significant P-value; SRMR values close to 0.08 or below; and RMSEA values close to 0.08 or below.

In order to conduct the CFA for measurement model, the software AMOS v.23 was used. The model showed an overall good fit and as a result the indices strongly support the measurement model's fit qualities ($X^2 = 1,766.063$, $p > 0.05$, RMSEA= 0.07, SRMR= 0.084).

4.4 REGRESSION ANALYSIS

Following the analysis of descriptive statistics, it is important to remember that the aim of this research is to investigate the emotional side of venture performance; in order to do so, the hypotheses within the theoretical framework consider positive and negative affect as well as EI and explain how these emotional components should be related to entrepreneurs' venture performance. Specifically, this study postulates that both positive and negative affect are positively related to venture performance (*H1* and *H2*); furthermore, it assumes that the two clusters of EI, self-awareness and self-management (Boyatzis, 2009), and more specifically the competences which belong to them (emotional self-awareness, emotional self-control, adaptability, achievement orientation, and positive outlook) have a positive effect on entrepreneurs' venture performance (*H3–H7*).

The results of regression analysis run using SPSS v.26 are reported in Table 4. In order to test the hypotheses, seven different models were designed and for each one all of the control variables (firm age and size; entrepreneurs' gender, age, and education level) were entered. Model 1 shows the main effect between positive affect and venture performance, with the results demonstrating that positive affect has a positive and significative influence over venture performance ($\beta = 0.20$; $p < 0.05$) and thus supports *H1*. In contrast, the data analysis does not support *H2*. Model 2 shows that negative affect does not have a significative effect on venture performance.

The next stage is to analyse the relationship between EI competencies and venture performance. Model 3 shows that emotional self-awareness does not have any significative impact on venture performance, meaning the data does not support *H3*. Model 4, considering the effect of positive outlook on venture performance, shows a significant association between these variables ($\beta = 0.22$; $p < 0.05$) and thus supports *H4*. Similarly, in terms of the extent to which the role of achievement orientation competence on venture performance, the results show the positive and significative association (see Model 6, $\beta = 0.23$; $p < 0.05$), thus providing evidence regarding *H6*. Moreover, looking at Model 5, the data shows that adaptability has a positive and strongly significant association with venture performance in such a way that the higher the adaptability, the stronger the impact on venture performance ($\beta = 0.42$; $p < 0.001$); there is therefore clear support for *H5*. Finally, Model 7 shows that emotional self-control does not have any significant effect on venture performance and consequently *H7* cannot be supported.

Among the control variables, firm size shows a significant effect on venture performance (Model 1: $\beta = 0.42$, $p < 0.05$; Model 2: $\beta = 0.45$, $p < 0.05$; Model 3: $\beta = 0.42$, $p < 0.05$; Model 4: $\beta = 0.42$; $p < 0.05$; Model 6: $\beta = 0.36$, $p < 0.05$; Model 7: $\beta = 0.44$, $p < 0.05$) with the exception of Model 5, which considers the relationship between adaptability and venture performance. Regarding the individual control variables, only the entrepreneurs' educational level shows significant results in all the model analysed (Model 1: $\beta = 0.15$, $p < 0.05$; Model 2: $\beta = 0.15$, $p < 0.05$; Model 3: $\beta = 0.16$, $p < 0.05$; Model 4: $\beta = 0.14$, $p < 0.05$; Model 5: $\beta = 0.13$, $p < 0.05$; Model 6: $\beta = 0.15$, $p < 0.05$; Model 7: $\beta = 0.15$; $p < 0.05$); in other words, the higher the entrepreneur's educational level, the stronger the impact on venture performance.

Finally, at the end of Table 4 the *F*-test results are shown. The *F*-test is used in regression analysis to test the hypothesis that all model parameters are 0.

Table 4. Results of the Regression Analysis on Venture Performance.

	Venture Performance						
	Model 1	Model 2	Model 3	Model 4	Model 5	Model 6	Model 7
Positive affect	0.20*						
	(2.008)						
Negative affect		−0.085					
		(−0.0815)					
Self-awareness			0.089				
			(0.866)				
Positive outlook				0.220*			
				(2.246)			
Adaptability					0.422***		
					(0.4.504)		
Achievement orientation						0.236*	
						(2.337)	
Self-control							0.023
							(0.226)
Firm age	0.002	0.002	0.002	0.002	0.004	0.003	0.001
	(0.633)	(0.458)	(0.496)	(0.661)	(1.260)	(0.771)	(0.400)
Firm size (N.Emp)	0.429*	0.450*	0.427*	0.420*	0.284	0.369*	0.447*
	(2.432)	(2.504)	(2.351)	(2.392)	(1.712)	(2.073)	(2.472)
Gender	−0.287	−0.307	−0.343	−0.302	−0.216	−0.381	−0.308
	(−1,208)	(−1,270)	(−1,411)	(−1,284)	(−0.986)	(−1.613)	(−1.250)
Entrepreneurs' age	0.006	0.001	0.003	0.003	0.000	0.005	0.003
	(0.730)	(0.101)	(0.354)	(0.325)	(0.049)	(0.580)	(0.334)
Educational level	0.151*	0.152*	0.160*	0.144*	0.131*	0.156*	0.150*
	(2.384)	(2.364)	(2.452)	(2.287)	(2.241)	(2.481)	(2.294)
R^2	0.205	0.173	0.174	0.463	0.329	0.218	0.167
Adj. R^2	0.148	0.114	0.115	0.158	0.281	0.162	0.108
F-test	3.612**	2.938**	2.955**	3.814**	6.863***	3.898**	2.815**

t-Statistics are within parentheses.

*$p < 0.05$, **$p < 0.01$, ***$p < 0.001$.

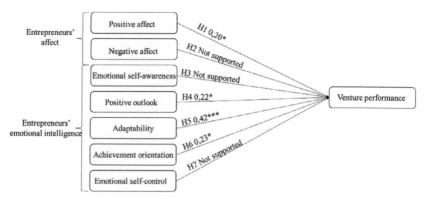

Source: Author's elaboration.

Fig. 6.   Summary of Supported and Not Supported Hypotheses.

It is also used in statistical analysis when comparing statistical models that have been fitted using the same underlying factors and dataset to determine the model with the best fit. The data shows that all the models are significative but, in line with regression analysis, the models with higher coefficients are the models which have significative results (i.e. Model 1: F-test = 3.61, $p < 0.01$; Model 4: F-test = 3.81, $p < 0.01$; Model 5: F-test = 6.86, $p < 0.001$; Model 6: F-test = 3.89, $p < 0.01$).

Fig. 6 exhibits a summary of the research model with the indication of the supported and not supported hypotheses.

4.5 MAIN FINDINGS

Regarding the affect component of the framework, the findings suggest that only positive affect has a positive and significative impact on venture performance (*H1*). Moreover, the findings related to the effect of negative affect and venture performance do not support the hypothesis regarding a positive and significative effect between these variables (*H2*). With regard to the role of EI competences and venture performance, the study postulates that the two clusters of EI, self-awareness and self-management (Boyatzis, 2009), and more specifically the competences which belong to them (emotional self-awareness, emotional self-control, adaptability, achievement orientation, and positive outlook) have a positive effect on entrepreneurs' venture performance (*H3–H7*).

In this regard, the findings demonstrate that the self-awareness cluster, specifically the self-awareness competence, had no significative effect on venture performance (*H3*). Moreover, considering the self-management cluster of competences, the findings showed that three out of four competences had a positive and significative effect on venture performance. Specifically, the analysis established that emotional self-control has no influence over venture performance (*H7*). However, achievement orientation and positive outlook have a positive and significative effect on venture performance (*H4* and *H6*). The strongest finding relates to the effect of adaptability competence and venture performance (*H5*). Finally, in general, the findings demonstrate that there are two control variables that should be considered when the emotional side of venture performance is investigated: the firm's size and the entrepreneur's educational level. It is important to note that the firm size has a significative effect when all the independent variables of the model are considered except for adaptability. This means that in all firms, whether large or small, entrepreneurs able to adapt and manage changes in order to not only survive but also achieve better venture performance.

In the light of these research findings, the main implications – both theoretical and practical – are presented in the following and last chapter of this book.

5

IMPLICATIONS AND MAIN CONCLUSION

5.1 CONCLUSION AND FINAL REMARKS

This contribution began with the necessity of considering emotions during discussions of entrepreneurial performance (Baron, 2008; Ingram et al., 2019; Lerner, Li, et al., 2015). The most recent studies have argued that entrepreneurial emotion is a 'hot topic' (Cardon et al., 2012); accordingly, research efforts show that emotions influence both opportunity evaluation and exploitation decision (Hayton & Cholakova, 2012; Welpe et al., 2012) and performance in general (Baron et al., 2012; Cardon et al., 2005). This is due to the fact that

> *entrepreneurship generates substantial emotions because it is an extreme context in terms of time pressures, uncertainty, and the extent of personal consequences tied up in the fate of the firm. (Cardon et al., 2012, p. 7)*

Indeed, entrepreneurship is a high emotional labour context where positive and negative affect have a critical role and where emotions have to be controlled in order to achieve higher performance (Cardon et al., 2012). Although scholars have begun to emphasise the role of emotion in entrepreneurial behaviour, this line of inquiry still needs to be understood in a more overarching way (Ingram et al., 2019).

Considering this literature gap, the author aimed to develop and test a theoretical framework to investigate the emotional side of venture performance. In order to do so, seven different hypotheses were discussed in Chapter 3 and an overarching theoretical framework about the emotional side of venture performance was developed. Specifically, the hypotheses considered affect, both positive and negative, and EI competences and explained how these emotional components should be related to entrepreneurs' venture performance. Specifically, this study postulates that both positive and negative affect are positively related to venture performance (*H1* and *H2*); moreover, it assumes that the two clusters of EI, self-awareness and self-management (Boyatzis, 2009), and more specifically the competences which belong to them (emotional self-awareness, emotional self-control, adaptability, achievement orientation, and positive outlook) have a positive effect on entrepreneurs' venture performance (*H3–H7*).

Regarding the affect component of the framework, the findings suggest that only positive affect has a positive and significative impact on venture performance (*H1*). This result confirms the previous studies regarding the benefits associated with experiencing PA for both individual and company performance (Delgado-García et al., 2012; Fodor & Pintea, 2017). However, the findings related to the effect of negative affect and venture performance do not support the hypothesis about a positive and significative effect between these variables (*H2*). Hence, the findings do not confirm the theory that when negative emotions are felt, people tend to perceive the overall situation as unfavourable and engage in detailed and careful analysis to avoid mistakes in an attempt to improve the current affective state (Elsbach & Barr, 1999; Sassetti et al., 2019). In contrast, the research results confirm the meta-analysis contribution by Fodor and Pintea (2017) who demonstrated that, overall, negative affect has no significant implications for entrepreneurial performance.

Moving onto the main findings regarding the role of EI competences and venture performance, it is important to remember that the theoretical framework postulated in this contribution is inspired by Boyatzis (2009) studies. The author explains that EI competencies are divided into two clusters. The self-awareness cluster concerns knowing one's internal states, preferences, resources, and intuitions and contains one competency: emotional self-awareness, which refers to recognising one's emotions and their effects. On the other hand, the self-management cluster refers to managing one's internal states, impulses, and resources. This cluster contains four competencies: emotional self-control, which refers to keeping disruptive emotions and impulses in check; adaptability, which refers to flexibility in handling change; achievement orientation, which involves striving to improve or meeting a standard of excellence; and positive outlook, which refers to seeing the positive aspects of things and the future.

To the best of the author's knowledge, there is no recent contribution which considers the EI competencies as theorised by Boyatzis (2009) as well as entrepreneurs' venture performance, even though previous research supports this hypothesis (Cross & Travaglione, 2003). For these reasons, the present study postulates that the two clusters of EI, self-awareness and self-management (Boyatzis, 2009), and more specifically the competences which belong to them (emotional self-awareness, emotional self-control, adaptability, achievement orientation, and positive outlook) have a positive effect on entrepreneurs' venture performance (*H3–H7*).

In this regard, the findings show that the self-awareness cluster, specifically the self-awareness competence, had no significative effect on venture performance (*H3*). This means that the entrepreneurs' ability to recognise emotions and their effects is not directly associated with venture performance. Instead, considering the self-management cluster of competences, the findings show that three out of four competences had a positive and significant effect on venture performance. The analysis has established that emotional self-control, that is, the entrepreneurs' ability to keep disruptive emotions and impulses in check has no effect on venture performance (*H7*). However, the entrepreneurs' emotional competences in terms of striving to improve or meeting a standard of excellence (achievement orientation) and seeing the positive aspects of things and the future (positive outlook) have a positive and significative effect on venture performance (*H4* and *H6*) . The strongest finding relates to the effect of adaptability competence and venture performance as the results indicate not only the positive effect of competence on the dependent variable but also that this relation is strongly significative (*H5*). This means that in order to achieve best venture performance, entrepreneurs predominantly need to be able to adapt and be flexible in handling change.

5.2 THEORETICAL CONTRIBUTION

From a theoretical point of view, this research intends to contribute to the existing understanding of the emotional side of entrepreneurs' venture performance. The literature review and the main findings have confirmed that as entrepreneurs personally identify with their ventures and constantly face the unknown, they are inherently likely to feel strong affect and emotions (Delgado García et al., 2015; Doern & Goss, 2013; Morris et al., 2012).

Specifically, this contribution confirms previous results regarding the benefits associated with experiencing positive affect for both individual and company performance (Delgado-García et al., 2012; Fodor & Pintea, 2017). At the same time, the findings also confirm that, overall, negative affect had no significant implications for entrepreneurial performance (Fodor & Pintea,

2017). The benefits of feeling good and positive are not just due to the fact that such feelings allow entrepreneurs to play down, ignore, or distort negative information; rather, they derive from the fact that positive affect helps entrepreneurs consider many aspects of a situation simultaneously, make evaluations, and choose appropriate behaviours in response to the situation and task demands (Lewis, 2011).

Moreover, this research contributes to entrepreneurship literature by also focussing on the relationship between EI competencies and venture performance. To the best of our knowledge, there is no recent contribution which links the EI competencies as theorised by Boyatzis (2009) and entrepreneurs' venture performance, even though previous research supports this hypothesis (Cross & Travaglione, 2003). Consequently, the findings of this book are the first attempt to demonstrate which EI competences differentiate entrepreneurs in terms of performance. The data analysis shows that the entrepreneurs' emotional competences about striving to improve or meeting a standard of excellence (achievement orientation) and seeing the positive aspects of things and the future (positive outlook) have a positive and significative effect on venture performance. The strongest finding relates to the effect of adaptability competence and venture performance; the results not only show the positive effect of the competence on the dependent variable but also provide evidence that this relation is highly significant.

Overall, from a theoretical point of view, this research contributes to entrepreneurship literature by demonstrating that entrepreneurs who have a positive state of mind, are oriented to achieve their goals, and are adaptable are more willing to explore venture alternatives and consequently attain better performance.

5.3 PRACTICAL IMPLICATIONS

The research findings may also have practical implications, mostly in the field of entrepreneurial educational programmes. Specifically, these training should encourage positive organisational behaviours such as the application of positively oriented human resource strengths and psychological capacities that can be measured, developed, and effectively managed for performance improvement in today's workplace. If entrepreneurs are able to develop their positive state there are also more likely to enhance teamwork, articulate a vision, encourage employee participation, treat people with respect, change the culture, become more customer-centric, establish stretch goals, and, more generally, establish an effective organisation (Cameron, 2012).

Moreover, it could be useful to support entrepreneurs in developing skills which enable them to anticipate the effects that emotions could have on their decisions and consequently on their performance (Fiori, 2009). From this perspective, it could be useful in developing the EI. Indeed, entrepreneurs may voluntarily practice, develop, and apply these abilities in specific situations. This means that entrepreneurs with a higher level of EI may be more adaptable in different situations (Fiori, 2009; Sassetti et al., 2019). Hence, one of the main findings of this research is that adaptability is the most significative impactful competence on venture performance. Indeed, in order to build adaptable organisations, firstly entrepreneurs have to be able to develop their adaptability and become leaders for organisational adaptability (Uhl-Bien & Arena, 2018). This differs from leading change in that, rather than focussing on how leaders can drive change from a top down perspective, for example, through vision and inspiration (Griffith, Connelly, Thiel, & Johnson, 2015; Margolis & Ziegert, 2016), it addresses how leaders can position organisations and the people within them to be adaptive in the face of complex challenges.

Research has also shown that leaders with high EI produce positive work attitudes and altruistic behaviours (Carmeli, 2003) and that their employees enjoy higher job satisfaction and performance (Wong & Law, 2002). Similarly, entrepreneurs with high EI can facilitate the performance of their employees by encouraging emotions that foster more creativity, produce resilience, and enable employees to act (Zhou & George, 2003). Furthermore, leaders with high EI should be more adept at nurturing more positive interactions between employees, which in turn could foster higher levels of cooperation (Barsade, 2002), coordination (Sy, Côté, & Saavedra, 2005), and organisational citizenship behaviours that contribute to performance (Wong & Law, 2002). Entrepreneurs may therefore be interested in implementing human resource strategies aimed at developing their own EI, for instance appropriate training courses. Entrepreneurs who are able to improve their understanding of their moods and emotions will make better decisions, avoiding biases and increasing their venture performance.

In order to improve the effectiveness of this learning process, it could be useful to develop games and simulations. These training techniques are experiential activities that place individuals in a microworld where they apply their knowledge, skills, and strategies in the execution of their own roles and achievement of the desired results. More specifically, during simulations individuals interact with real-world settings, addressing issues, threats, and different problems that arise in the situation according to an ever evolving scenario. Nonetheless, the most valuable characteristic is the fact that during simulations, participants receive realistic feedback on their actions via a change in the status of the problem addressed and via reactions from other players. All in all, the better the fit between the real life and the simulation setting, the greater the validity and learning value of the simulation (Alessi, 2000) Previous data has already highlighted the efficiency of gaming/simulations in developing new skills, raising awareness and motivation, or providing knowledge and insight (Geurts, de Caluwé, & Stoppelenburg, 2000). Gaming and simulation could also contribute to the entrepreneurs' personal development by revealing gaps in their knowledge, weaknesses related to their skills, and strategies related to their performance.

REFERENCES

Aguinis, H., Ramani, R. S., & Alabduljader, N. (2018). What you see is what you get? Enhancing methodological transparency in management research. *Academy of Management Annals, 12*(1), 83–110. doi:doi.org/10.5465/annals.2016.0011

Ahmetoglu, G., Leutner, F., & Chamorro-Premuzic, T. (2011). EQ-nomics: Understanding the relationship between individual differences in trait emotional intelligence and entrepreneurship. *Personality and Individual Differences, 51*(8), 1028–1033. doi:doi.org/10.1016/j.paid.2011.08.016

Alessi, S. (2000). Designing educational support in system-dynamics-based interactive learning environments. *Simulation & Gaming, 31*(2), 178–196. doi:doi.org/10.1177/104687810003100205

Ashby, F. G., & Isen, A. M. (1999). A neuropsychological theory of positive affect and its influence on cognition. *Psychological Review, 106*(3), 529. doi:doi.org/10.1037/0033-295X.106.3.529

Awwad, M. S., & Ali, H. K. (2012). Emotional intelligence and entrepreneurial orientation. *Journal of Research in Marketing and Entrepreneurship, 14*(1), 115. doi:doi.org/10.1108/14715201211246869

Baron, R. A. (2007). Behavioral and cognitive factors in entrepreneurship: Entrepreneurs as the active element in new venture creation. *Strategic Entrepreneurship Journal, 1*(1–2), 167–182. doi:doi.org/10.1002/sej.12

Baron, R. A. (2008). The role of affect in the entrepreneurial process. *Academy of Management Review, 33*(2), 328–340. doi:doi.org/10.5465/amr.2008.31193166

Baron, R. A. (2015). Affect and entrepreneurship. *Wiley Encyclopedia of Management, 3*, 1–3. doi:doi.org/10.1002/9781118785317.weom030002

Baron, R. A., Hmieleski, K. M., & Henry, R. A. (2012). Entrepreneurs' dispositional positive affect: The potential benefits – and potential costs – of being "up". *Journal of Business Venturing, 27*(3), 310–324. doi:doi.org/10.1016/j.jbusvent.2011.04.002

Baron, R. A., & Tang, J. (2011). The role of entrepreneurs in firm-level innovation: Joint effects of positive affect, creativity, and environmental dynamism. *Journal of Business Venturing, 26*(1), 49–60. doi:doi.org/10.1016/j.jbusvent.2009.06.002

Bar-On, R. (1997). *BarOn emotional quotient inventory.* North Tonawanda, NY: Multi-health systems.

Baron, R. A., Tang, J., & Hmieleski, K. M. (2011). The downside of being 'up': entrepreneurs' dispositional positive affect and firm performance. *Strategic Entrepreneurship Journal, 5*(2), 101–119. doi:10.1002/sej.109

Bar-On, R. (2004). The Bar-On Emotional Quotient Inventory (EQ-i): Rationale, description and summary of psychometric properties. In G. Geher (Ed.), *Measuring emotional intelligence: Common ground and controversy* (pp. 115–145). New York, NY: Nova Science Publishers.

Bar-On, R. E., & Parker, J. D. (2000). *The handbook of emotional intelligence: Theory, development, assessment, and application at home, school, and in the workplace.* San Francisco, CA: Jossey-Bass.

Barsade, S. G. (2002). The ripple effect: Emotional contagion and its influence on group behavior. *Administrative Science Quarterly, 47*(4), 644–675. doi:doi.org/10.2307/3094912

Barsky, A., Thoresen, C. J., Warren, C. R., & Kaplan, S. A. (2004). Modeling negative affectivity and job stress: A contingency-based approach. *Journal of Organizational Behavior: The International Journal of Industrial, Occupational and Organizational Psychology and Behavior, 25*(8), 915–936. doi:doi.org/10.1002/job.285

Baum, J. R., & Locke, E. A. (2004). The relationship of entrepreneurial traits, skill, and motivation to subsequent venture growth. *Journal of Applied Psychology, 89*(4), 587. doi:doi.org/10.1037/0021-9010.89.4.587

Bernoster, I., Mukerjee, J., & Thurik, R. (2020). The role of affect in entrepreneurial orientation. *Small Business Economics, 54*(1), 235–256. doi:doi.org/10.1007/s11187-018-0116-3

Binet, A. (1905). A propos la mesure de l' intelligence. *L' Annee Psychology, 2,* 411–465.

Birley, S., & Westhead, P. (1990). Growth and performance contrasts between 'types' of small firms. *Strategic Management Journal, 11*(7), 535–557. doi:doi.org/10.1002/smj.4250110705

Breugst, N., & Shepherd, D. A. (2017). If you fight with me, I'll get mad! A social model of entrepreneurial affect. *Entrepreneurship Theory and Practice, 41*(3), 379–418. doi:10.1111/etap.12211

Boyatzis, R. E. (1982). *The competent manager: A model for effective performance.* Hoboken, NJ: John Wiley & Sons.

Boyatzis, R. E. (2006). Using tipping points of emotional intelligence and cognitive competencies to predict financial performance of leaders. *Psicothema, 18*, 124–131.

Boyatzis, R. E. (2007). Developing emotional intelligence competencies. In *Applying emotional intelligence: A practitioner's guide* (pp. 28–52).

Boyatzis, R. E. (2008). Leadership development from a complexity perspective. *Consulting Psychology Journal: Practice and Research, 60*(4), 298. doi:doi.org/10.1037/1065-9293.60.4.298

Boyatzis, R. E. (2009). Competencies as a behavioral approach to emotional intelligence. *Journal of Management Development, 28*(9), 749–770. doi:doi.org/10.1108/02621710910987647

Boyatzis, R. E., Gaskin, J., & Wei, H. (2015). Emotional and social intelligence and behavior. In Springer (Ed.), *Handbook of intelligence* (pp. 243–262). New York, NY: Springer.

Boyatzis, R. E., Goleman, D., & Rhee, K. (2000). Clustering competence in emotional intelligence: Insights from the Emotional Competence Inventory (ECI). *Handbook of Emotional Intelligence, 99*(6), 343–362.

Boyatzis, R. E., & Ratti, F. (2009). Emotional, social and cognitive intelligence competencies distinguishing effective Italian managers and leaders in a private company and cooperatives. *Journal of Management Development, 28*(9), 821–838. https://doi.org/10.1108/02621710910987674

Boyatzis, R. E., & Sala, F. (2004). Assessing emotional intelligence competencies. *The Measurement of Emotional Intelligence,* 147–180.

Brackett, M. A., Mayer, J. D., & Warner, R. M. (2004). Emotional intelligence and its relation to everyday behaviour. *Personality and Individual Differences, 36*(6), 1387–1402. doi:doi.org/10.1016/S0191-8869(03)00236-8

Breugst, N., Domurath, A., Patzelt, H., & Klaukien, A. (2012). Perceptions of entrepreneurial passion and employees' commitment to entrepreneurial ventures. *Entrepreneurship Theory and Practice, 36*(1), 171–192. doi:doi.org/10.1111/j.1540-6520.2011.00491.x

Brigham, K. H., De Castro, J. O., & Shepherd, D. A. (2007). A person–organization fit model of owner–managers' cognitive style and organizational demands. *Entrepreneurship Theory and Practice, 31*(1), 29–51. doi:doi.org/10.1111/j.1540-6520.2007.00162.x

Brown, T. A. (2006). *Confirmatory factor analysis for applied research.* New York, NY: Guilford Press.

Brown, T. A., & Moore, M. T. (2012). Confirmatory factor analysis. In R. H. Hoyle (Ed.), *Handbook of structural equation modeling.* New York, NY: Guilford Press.

Brundin, E., & Gustafsson, V. (2013). Entrepreneurs' decision making under different levels of uncertainty: The role of emotions. *International Journal of Entrepreneurial Behaviour & Research, 19*(6), 568–591. doi:doi.org/10.1108/IJEBR-07-2012-0074

Brundin, E., Wigren, C., Isaacs, E., Friedrich, C., & Visser, K. (2008). Triple helix networks in a multicultural context: Triggers and barriers for fostering growth and sustainability. *Journal of Developmental Entrepreneurship, 13*(01), 77–98. doi:doi.org/10.1142/S1084946708000867

Brush, C. G., & Vanderwerf, P. A. (1992). A comparison of methods and sources for obtaining estimates of new venture performance. *Journal of Business Venturing, 7*(2), 157–170. doi:doi.org/10.1016/0883-9026(92)90010-O

Cameron, K. (1978). Measuring organizational effectiveness in institutions of higher education. *Administrative Science Quarterly, 23,* 604–632. doi:doi.org/10.2307/2392582

Cameron, K. (2012). *Positive leadership: Strategies for extraordinary performance.* San Francisco, CA: Berrett-Koehler Publishers.

Cantillon, R. (1755). *Essai sur la nature du commerce en général (The nature of trade in general).* Paris: Institut National D'études Démographiques.

Cardon, M. S. (2008). Is passion contagious? The transference of entrepreneurial passion to employees. *Human Resource Management Review, 18*(2), 77–86. doi:doi.org/10.1016/j.hrmr.2008.04.001

Cardon, M. S., Foo, M. D., Shepherd, D., & Wiklund, J. (2012). Exploring the heart: Entrepreneurial emotion is a hot topic. *Entrepreneurship Theory and Practice, 36*(1), 1–10. doi:doi.org/10.1111/j.1540-6520.2011.00501.x

Cardon, M. S., & Kirk, C. P. (2015). Entrepreneurial passion as mediator of the self-efficacy to persistence relationship. *Entrepreneurship Theory and Practice, 39*(5), 1027–1050. doi:doi.org/10.1111/etap.12089

Cardon, M. S., Wincent, J., Singh, J., & Drnovsek, M. (2005, August). Entrepreneurial passion: The nature of emotions in entrepreneurship. In *Academy of Management Proceedings* (Vol. 2005, No. 1, pp. G1–G6). Briarcliff Manor, NY: Academy of Management.

Cardon, M. S., Wincent, J., Singh, J., & Drnovsek, M. (2009). The nature and experience of entrepreneurial passion. *Academy of Management Review, 34*(3), 511–532. doi:doi.org/10.5465/amr.2009.40633190

Carmeli, A. (2003). The relationship between emotional intelligence and work attitudes, behavior and outcomes: An examination among senior managers. *Journal of Managerial Psychology, 18*(8), 788–813. doi:doi.org/10.1108/02683940310511881

Carver, C. S., & Scheier, M. F. (1990). Origins and functions of positive and negative affect: A control-process view. *Psychological Review, 97*(1), 19. doi:doi.org/10.1037/0033-295X.97.1.19

Cattell, R. B. (1971). *Abilities: Their structure, growth, and action.* Boston, MA: Houghton Mifflin.

Chan, Y. C., Lam, G. L. T., Chun, P. K. R., & So, M. T. E. (2006). Confirmatory factor analysis of the Child Abuse Potential Inventory: Results based on a sample of Chinese mothers in Hong Kong. *Child Abuse & Neglect, 30*, 1005–1016. doi:doi.org/10.1037/0033-295X.97.1.19

Chen, X. P., Yao, X., & Kotha, S. (2009). Entrepreneur passion and preparedness in business plan presentations: A persuasion analysis of venture capitalists' funding decisions. *Academy of Management Journal, 52*(1), 199–214. doi:doi.org/10.5465/amj.2009.36462018

Cherniss, C. (2010). Emotional intelligence: Toward clarification of a concept. *Industrial and Organizational Psychology, 3*(2), 110–126. doi:10.1111/j.1754-9434.2010.01231.x

Cherniss, C., & Adler, M. (2000). *Promoting emotional intelligence in organizations: Make training in emotional intelligence effective.* Alexandria, VA: American Society for Training and Development.

Clarke, J. (2011). Revitalizing entrepreneurship: How visual symbols are used in entrepreneurial performances. *Journal of Management Studies, 48*(6), 1365–1391. doi:doi.org/10.1111/j.1467-6486.2010.01002.x

Clore, G. L. (1992). Cognitive phenomenology: Feelings and the construction of judgment. *The Construction of Social Judgments, 10*, 133–163.

Clore, G. L., Schwarz, N., & Conway, M. (1994). Affective causes and consequences of social information processing. In R. S. Wyer, Jr. & T. K. Srull (Eds.), *Handbook of social cognition: Basic processes; Applications* (pp. 323–417). Mahwah, NJ: Lawrence Erlbaum Associates, Inc.

Cooper, A. C. (1993). Challenges in predicting new firm performance. *Journal of Business Venturing, 8*(3), 241–253. doi:doi.org/10.1016/0883-9026(93)90030-9

Covin, J. G., & Slevin, D. P. (1991). A conceptual model of entrepreneurship as firm behavior. *Entrepreneurship Theory and Practice, 16*(1), 7–26. doi:doi.org/10.1177/104225879101600102

Crawford, J. R., & Henry, J. D. (2004). The Positive and Negative Affect Schedule (PANAS): Construct validity, measurement properties and normative data in a large non-clinical sample. *British Journal of Clinical Psychology, 43*(3), 245–265. doi:doi.org/10.1348/0144665031752934

Cross, B., & Travaglione, A. (2003). The untold story: Is the entrepreneur of the 21st century defined by emotional intelligence? *International Journal of Organizational Analysis, 11*(3), 221. doi:doi.org/10.1108/eb028973

Delgado García, J. B., De Quevedo Puente, E., & Blanco Mazagatos, V. (2015). How affect relates to entrepreneurship: A systematic review of the literature and research agenda. *International Journal of Management Reviews, 17*(2), 191–211. doi:doi.org/10.1111/ijmr.12058

Delgado-García, J. B., Rodríguez-Escudero, A. I., & Martín-Cruz, N. (2012). Influence of affective traits on entrepreneur's goals and satisfaction. *Journal of Small Business Management, 50*(3), 408–428. doi:doi.org/10.1111/j.1540-627X.2012.00359.x

DeVellis, R. F. (2016). *Scale development: Theory and applications* (Vol. 26). Thousand Oaks, CA: Sage Publications.

Dewald, J., & Bowen, F. (2010). Storm clouds and silver linings: Responding to disruptive innovations through cognitive resilience. *Entrepreneurship Theory and Practice, 34*(1), 197–218. doi:doi.org/10.1111/j.1540-6520.2009.00312.x

Dijkhuizen, J., Gorgievski, M., van Veldhoven, M., & Schalk, R. (2016). Feeling successful as an entrepreneur: A job demands–resources approach.

International Entrepreneurship and Management Journal, 12(2), 555–573. doi:doi.org/10.1007/s11365-014-0354-z

Dillman, D. A., Smyth, J. D., & Christian, L. M. (2014). *Internet, phone, mail, and mixed-mode surveys: The tailored design method.* Hoboken, NJ: John Wiley & Sons.

Doern, R., & Goss, D. (2013). From barriers to barring: Why emotion matters for entrepreneurial development. *International Small Business Journal, 31*(5), 496–519. doi:doi.org/10.1177/0266242611425555

Doern, R., & Goss, D. (2014). The role of negative emotions in the social processes of entrepreneurship: Power rituals and shame-related appeasement behaviors. *Entrepreneurship Theory and Practice, 38*(4), 863–890. doi:doi.org/10.1111/etap.12026

Elsbach, K. D., & Barr, P. S. (1999). The effects of mood on individuals' use of structured decision protocols. *Organization Science, 10*(2), 181–198. doi:doi.org/10.1287/orsc.10.2.181

Elzahar, H., Hussainey, K., Mazzi, F., & Tsalavoutas, I. (2015). Economic consequences of key performance indicators' disclosure quality. *International Review of Financial Analysis, 39*, 96–112. doi:doi.org/10.1016/j.irfa.2015.03.005

Endres, A. M., & Woods, C. R. (2006). Modern theories of entrepreneurial behavior: A comparison and appraisal. *Small Business Economics, 26*(2), 189–202. doi:doi.org/10.1007/s11187-004-5608-7

Fan, W., & Yan, Z. (2010). Factors affecting response rates of the web survey: A systematic review. *Computers in Human Behavior, 26*(2), 132–139. doi:doi.org/10.1016/j.chb.2009.10.015

Fillenbaum, S., & Rapoport, A. (1970). *Emotion names. Studies in the Subjective Lexicon.* New York, NY: Academic Press.

Fiori, M. (2009). A new look at emotional intelligence: A dual-process framework. *Personality and Social Psychology Review, 13*(1), 21–44. doi:doi.org/10.1177/1088868308326909

Fodor, O. C., & Pintea, S. (2017). The "emotional side" of entrepreneurship: A meta-analysis of the relation between positive and negative affect and entrepreneurial performance. *Frontiers in Psychology, 8*, 310. doi:doi.org/10.3389/fpsyg.2017.00310

Foo, M. D. (2011). Emotions and entrepreneurial opportunity evaluation. *Entrepreneurship Theory and Practice, 35*(2), 375–393. doi:doi.org/10.1111/j.1540-6520.2009.00357.x

Foo, M. D., Murnieks, C. Y., & Chan, E. T. (2014). Feeling and thinking: The role of affect in entrepreneurial cognition. In *Handbook of entrepreneurial cognition*. London: Edward Elgar Publishing.

Foo, M. D., Uy, M. A., & Baron, R. A. (2009). How do feelings influence effort? An empirical study of entrepreneurs' affect and venture effort. *Journal of Applied Psychology, 94*(4), 1086. doi:doi.org/10.1037/a0015599

Forgas, J. P. (1995). Mood and judgment: The affect infusion model (AIM). *Psychological Bulletin, 117*(1), 39. doi:doi.org/10.1037/0033-2909.117.1.39

Forgas, J. P. (2000). Affect and information processing strategies: An interactive relationship. In J. P. Forgas (Ed.), *Studies in emotion and social interaction, second series. Feeling and thinking: The role of affect in social cognition* (pp. 253–280). Cambridge: Cambridge University Press.

Forgas, J. P., & George, J. M. (2001). Affective influences on judgments and behavior in organizations: An information processing perspective. *Organizational Behavior and Human Decision Processes, 86*(1), 3–34. doi:doi.org/10.1006/obhd.2001.2971

Frijda, N. H. (1993). The place of appraisal in emotion. *Cognition & Emotion, 7*(3–4), 357–387.

Gardner, H. E. (2000). *Intelligence reframed: Multiple intelligences for the 21st century*. London: Hachette UK.

Gartner, W. B. (1988). "Who is an entrepreneur?" is the wrong question. *American Journal of Small Business, 12*(4), 11–32. doi:doi.org/10.1177/104225878801200401

Geurts, J. L. A., de Caluwé, L. I. A., & Stoppelenburg, A. (2000). *Changing organisations with gaming/simulation*. New York, NY: Elsevier.

Goleman, D. (1995). *Emotional intelligence*. New York, NY: Bantam Books.

Goleman, D. (1998). *Working with emotional intelligence*. New York, NY: Bantam Books.

Goleman, D., Boyatzis, R., & McKee, A. (2002). The emotional reality of teams. *Journal of Organizational Excellence, 21*(2), 55–65. doi:doi.org/10.1002/npr.10020

Goleman, D., Boyatzis, R. E., & McKee, A. (2013). *Primal leadership: Unleashing the power of emotional intelligence*. Cambridge, MA: Harvard Business Press.

Grichnik, D., Smeja, A., & Welpe, I. (2010). The importance of being emotional: How do emotions affect entrepreneurial opportunity evaluation and exploitation? *Journal of Economic Behavior & Organization, 76*(1), 15–29. doi:doi.org/10.1016/j.jebo.2010.02.010

Griffith, J., Connelly, S., Thiel, C., & Johnson, G. (2015). How outstanding leaders lead with affect: An examination of charismatic, ideological, and pragmatic leaders. *The Leadership Quarterly, 26*(4), 502–517. doi:doi.org/10.1016/j.leaqua.2015.03.004

Hahn, V. C., Frese, M., Binnewies, C., & Schmitt, A. (2012). Happy and proactive? The role of hedonic and eudaimonic well-being in business owners' personal initiative. *Entrepreneurship Theory and Practice, 36*(1), 97–114. doi:doi.org/10.1111/j.1540-6520.2011.00490.x

Harrington, D. (2009). *Confirmatory factor analysis.* Oxford: Oxford University Press.

Hayton, J. C., & Cholakova, M. (2012). The role of affect in the creation and intentional pursuit of entrepreneurial ideas. *Entrepreneurship Theory and Practice, 36*(1), 41–67. doi:doi.org/10.1111/j.1540-6520.2011.00458.x

Hess, J. D., & Bacigalupo, A. C. (2011). Enhancing decisions and decision-making processes through the application of emotional intelligence skills. *Management Decision, 49*(5), 21. https://doi.org/10.1108/00251741111130805

Hess, J. D., & Bacigalupo, A. C. (2013). Applying emotional intelligence skills to leadership and decision making in non-profit organizations. *Administrative Sciences, 3*(4), 202–220. doi:doi.org/10.3390/admsci3040202

Hmieleski, K. M., & Baron, R. A. (2009). Entrepreneurs' optimism and new venture performance: A social cognitive perspective. *Academy of Management Journal, 52*(3), 473–488. doi:doi.org/10.5465/amj.2009.41330755

Ho, V. T., & Pollack, J. M. (2014). Passion isn't always a good thing: Examining entrepreneurs' network centrality and financial performance with a dualistic model of passion. *Journal of Management Studies, 51*(3), 433–459. doi:doi.org/10.1111/joms.12062

Hoffmann, T. (1999). The meanings of competency. *Journal of European Industrial Training, 23*(6), 275–285. doi:doi.org/10.1108/03090599910284650

Hu, L, & Bender, P. M. (1999). Cutoff criteria for fit indexes in covariance structure analysis: Conventional criteria versus new alternatives. *Structural Equation Modeling*, 6, 1–55. doi:doi.org/10.1080/10705519909540118

Ingram, A., Peake, W. O., Stewart, W., & Watson, W. (2019). Emotional intelligence and venture performance. *Journal of Small Business Management*, 57(3), 780–800. doi:doi.org/10.1111/jsbm.12333

IRPET. (2016). La situazione Economica e Sociale in Toscana. *Consuntivo 2015*. Retrieved from http://www.irpet.it

Janovics, J., & Christiansen, N. D. (2001, April). Emotional intelligence in the workplace. In *16th Annual conference of the society of industrial and organizational psychology*, San Diego, CA (pp. 26–29).

Jia, F., & Zhang, Y. (2018). The impact of positive affect on entrepreneurial motivational outcomes: A self-regulatory perspective. *International Review of Entrepreneurship*, 16(4), 627–656.

Kaufman, A. S., & Kaufman, J. C. (2001). Emotional intelligence as an aspect of general intelligence: What would David Wechsler say? *Emotion (Washington, DC)*, 1(3), 258–264.

Kaufmann, G., & Vosburg, S. K. (1997). "Paradoxical" mood effects on creative problem-solving. *Cognition and Emotion*, 11(2), 151–170. doi:doi.org/10.1080/026999397379971

Kennedy, P. (1985). *A guide to econometrics* (2nd ed.). Oxford: Basil Blackwell Ltd.

Kerr, R., Garvin, J., Heaton, N., & Boyle, E. (2006). Emotional intelligence and leadership effectiveness. *Leadership and Organization Development Journal*, 27(4), 265–279. doi:doi.org/10.1108/01437730610666028

Kirzner, I. M. (1979). *Perception, opportunity, and profit: Studies in the theory of entrepreneurship*. Chicago, IL: University of Chicago Press.

Kline, R. B. (2015). *Principles and practice of structural equation modeling*. New York, NY: Guilford Publications.

Kuratko, D. F. (2007). Entrepreneurial leadership in the 21st century: Guest editor's perspective. *Journal of Leadership & Organizational Studies*, 13(4), 1–11. doi:doi.org/10.1177/10717919070130040201

Kuratko, D. F., Ireland, R. D., Covin, J. G., & Hornsby, J. S. (2005). A model of middle-level managers' entrepreneurial behavior. *Entrepreneurship Theory and Practice*, 29(6), 699–716. doi:doi.org/10.1111/j.1540-6520.2005.00104.x

Kuvaas, B., & Kaufmann, G. (2004). Impact of mood, framing, and need for cognition on decision makers' recall and confidence. *Journal of Behavioral Decision Making, 17*(1), 59–74. doi:doi.org/10.1002/bdm.461

Langhorn, S. (2004). How emotional intelligence can improve management performance. *International Journal of Contemporary Hospitality Management, 16*(4), 220–230. doi:doi.org/10.1108/09596110410537379

Lerner, J. S., & Keltner, D. (2000). Beyond valence: Toward a model of emotion-specific influences on judgement and choice. *Cognition & Emotion, 14*(4), 473–493. doi:doi.org/10.1080/026999300402763

Lerner, J. S., Li, Y., Valdesolo, P., & Kassam, K. S. (2015). Emotion and decision making. *Annual Review of Psychology, 66*, 799-823. doi:doi.org/10.1146/annurev-psych-010213-115043

Lewis, S. (2011). *Positive psychology at work: How positive leadership and appreciative inquiry create inspiring organizations.* Hoboken, NJ: John Wiley & Sons.

Locke, E. A., & Latham, G. P. (1990). *A theory of goal setting & task performance.* Upper Saddle River, NJ: Prentice-Hall, Inc.

Lopes, P. N., Salovey, P., & Straus, R. (2003). Emotional intelligence, personality, and the perceived quality of social relationships. *Personality and individual Differences, 35*(3), 641–658. doi:doi.org/10.1016/S0191-8869(02)00242-8

Lumpkin, G. T., & Dess, G. G. (1996). Clarifying the entrepreneurial orientation construct and linking it to performance. *Academy of Management Review, 21*(1), 135–172. doi:doi.org/10.5465/amr.1996.9602161568

MacCann, C., Roberts, R. D., Matthews, G., & Zeidner, M. (2004). Consensus scoring and empirical option weighting of performance-based emotional intelligence (EI) tests. *Personality and Individual differences, 36*(3), 645–662. doi:doi.org/10.1016/S0191-8869(03)00123-5

Mair, J. (2005) Entrepreneurial behaviour in a large traditional firm: Exploring key drivers. In T. Elfring (Ed.), *Corporate entrepreneurship and venturing* (pp. 49–72). New York, NY: Springer.

Margolis, J. A., & Ziegert, J. C. (2016). Vertical flow of collectivistic leadership: An examination of the cascade of visionary leadership across levels. *The Leadership Quarterly, 27*(2), 334–348. doi:doi.org/10.1016/j.leaqua.2016.01.005

Markman, G. D., Balkin, D. B., & Baron, R. A. (2002). Inventors and new venture formation: The effects of general self-efficacy and regretful thinking. Entrepreneurship *Theory and Practice*, 27(2), 149–165. doi:10.1111/1540-8520.00004

Marshall, A. (1930). *Principles of economics*. London: Macmillan.

Matthews, G., Emo, A. K., Funke, G., Zeidner, M., Roberts, R. D., Costa, P. T., Jr, & Schulze, R. (2006). Emotional intelligence, personality, and task-induced stress. *Journal of Experimental Psychology: Applied*, 12(2), 96. doi:doi.org/10.1037/1076-898X.12.2.96

Maula, M., & Stam, W. (2020). Enhancing rigor in quantitative entrepreneurship research. *Entrepreneurship Theory and Practice*, 44(6), 1059–1090. doi:doi.org/10.1177/1042258719891388

Mayer, J. D., Caruso, D. R., & Salovey, P. (1999). Emotional intelligence meets traditional standards for an intelligence. *Intelligence*, 27(4), 267–298. https://doi.org/10.1016/S0160-2896(99)00016-1

Mayer, J. D., DiPaolo, M., & Salovey, P. (1990). Perceiving affective content in ambiguous visual stimuli: A component of emotional intelligence. *Journal of Personality Assessment*, 54(3–4), 772–781. doi:doi.org/10.1080/0022389 1.1990.9674037

Mayer, J. D., & Salovey, P. (1997). What is emotional intelligence. *Emotional Development and Emotional Intelligence: Educational Implications*, 3, 31.

Mayer, J. D., Salovey, P., & Caruso, D. R. (2000). Emotional intelligence as zeitgeist, as personality, and as a mental ability. In R. Bar-On & J. D. A. Parker (Eds.), *The handbook of emotional intelligence: Theory, development, assessment, and application at home, school, and in the workplace* (pp. 92–117). San Francisco, CA: Jossey-Bass.

Mayer, J. D., Salovey, P., & Caruso, D. R. (2002). Mayer–Salovey–Caruso emotional intelligence test (MSCEIT) item booklet.

Mayer, J. D., Salovey, P., & Caruso, D. R. (2004). Emotional intelligence: Theory, findings, and implications. *Psychological Inquiry*, 15(3), 197–215. doi:10.1207/s15327965pli1503_02

Mayer-Haug, K., Read, S., Brinckmann, J., Dew, N., & Grichnik, D. (2013). Entrepreneurial talent and venture performance: A meta-analytic investigation of SMEs. *Research Policy*, 42(6–7), 1251–1273. doi:doi.org/10.1016/j.respol.2013.03.001

McClelland, D. C. (1951). *Personality.* New York, NY: William Sloane Associates.

McKenzie, B., Ugbah, S. D., & Smothers, N. (2007). "Who Is an Entrepreneur?" Is it still the wrong question? *Academy of Entrepreneurship Journal, 13*(1), 23–43.

McMullen, J. S., & Shepherd, D. A. (2003). Extending the theory of the entrepreneur using a signal detection framework. In *Cognitive Approaches to Entrepreneurship Research.* London: Emerald Group Publishing Limited.

McMullen, J. S., & Shepherd, D. A. (2006). Entrepreneurial action and the role of uncertainty in the theory of the entrepreneur. *Academy of Management Review, 31*(1), 132–152. doi:doi.org/10.5465/amr.2006.19379628

Mill, J. (1848). *Principles of political economy with some of their application to social philosophy.* London: John W. Parker.

Mitchell, R. K., Busenitz, L., Lant, T., McDougall, P. P., Morse, E. A., & Smith, J. B. (2002). Toward a theory of entrepreneurial cognition: Rethinking the people side of entrepreneurship research. *Entrepreneurship Theory and Practice, 27*(2), 93–104. doi:doi.org/10.1111/1540-8520.00001

Mitchell, R. K., Busenitz, L. W., Bird, B., Marie Gaglio, C., McMullen, J. S., Morse, E. A., & Smith, J. B. (2007). The central question in entrepreneurial cognition research 2007. *Entrepreneurship Theory and Practice, 31*(1), 1–27. doi:doi.org/10.1111/j.1540-6520.2007.00161.x

Morris, M. H., Kuratko, D. F., Schindehutte, M., & Spivack, A. J. (2012). Framing the entrepreneurial experience. *Entrepreneurship Theory and Practice, 36*(1), 11–40. doi:doi.org/10.1111/j.1540-6520.2011.00471.x

Mortan, R. A., Ripoll, P., Carvalho, C., & Bernal, M. C. (2014). Effects of emotional intelligence on entrepreneurial intention and self-efficacy. *Revista de Psicología del Trabajo y de las Organizaciones, 30*(3), 97–104. doi:doi.org/10.1016/j.rpto.2014.11.004

Muyia, H. M. (2009). Approaches to and instruments for measuring emotional intelligence: A review of selected literature. *Advances in Developing Human Resources, 11*(6), 690–702. doi:doi.org/10.1177/1523422309360843

Ngah, R., & Salleh, Z. (2015). Emotional intelligence and entrepreneurs' innovativeness towards entrepreneurial success: A preliminary study. *American Journal of Economics, 5*(2), 285–290. doi:doi.org/10.5923/c.economics.201501.37

Nunnally, J. C. (1978). An Overview of psychological measurement. In B. B. Wolman (Ed.), *Clinical diagnosis of mental disorders: A handbook* (pp. 97–146). New York, NY: Plenum.

Randolph-Seng, B., Mitchell, R. K., Vahidnia, H., Mitchell, J. R., Chen, S., & Statzer, J. (2015). *The microfoundations of entrepreneurial cognition research: Toward an integrative approach. Foundations and Trends in Entrepreneurship*, 11(4),207–335.

Robinson, P. B., Stimpson, D. V., Huefner, J. C., & Hunt, H. K. (1991). An attitude approach to the prediction of entrepreneurship. *Entrepreneurship Theory and Practice*, 15(4), 13–32. doi:10.1177/104225879101500405

Salovey, P., Bedell, B. T., Detweiler, J. B., & Mayer, J. D. (1999). Coping intelligently: Emotional intelligence and the coping process. In C. R. Snyder (Ed.), *Coping: The psychology of what works* (pp. 141–164). New York, NY: Oxford University Press.

Salovey, P., & Grewal, D. (2005). The science of emotional intelligence. *Current Directions in Psychological Science*, 14(6), 281–285. doi:doi.org/10.1111/j.0963-7214.2005.00381.x

Salovey, P., & Mayer, J. D. (1990). Emotional intelligence. *Imagination, Cognition and Personality*, 9(3), 185–211. doi:doi.org/10.2190/DUGG-P24E-52WK-6CDG

Sassetti, S., Cavaliere, V., & Lombardi, S. (2019). Entrepreneurial success: A theoretical contribution linking affect and cognition. In Springer (Ed.), *The anatomy of entrepreneurial decisions* (pp. 57–77). Cham: Springer.

Sassetti, S., Marzi, G., Cavaliere, V., & Ciappei, C. (2018). Entrepreneurial cognition and socially situated approach: A systematic and bibliometric analysis. *Scientometrics*, 116(3), 1675–1718. https://doi.org/10.1007/s11192-018-2809-4

Say, J. B. (1846 [1964]). *Traité d'économie politique: ou, simple exposition de la manière dont se forment, se distribuent et se consomment les richesses [Treatise on political economy: On the production, distribution and consumption of wealth]* (1st ed.: 1827). New York, NY: Kelley.

Schaffer, L. F., Gilmer, B., & Schoen, M. (1940). *Psychology* (p. xii). New York, NY: Harper & Brothers.

Schumpeter, J. A., & Nichol, A. J. (1934). Robinson's economics of imperfect competition. *Journal of Political Economy*, 42(2), 249–259.

Schwarz, N. (2000). Emotion, cognition, and decision making. *Cognition & Emotion, 14*(4), 433–440. doi:doi.org/10.1080/026999300402745

Schwarz, N., & Clore, G. L. (1996). Feelings and phenomenal experiences. In E. T. Higgins & A. W. Kruglanski (Eds.), *Social psychology: Handbook of basic principles* (pp. 433–465). New York, NY: The Guilford Press.

Sciascia, S., & De Vita, R. (2004). *The development of entrepreneurship research*. Castellanza: Università Carlo Cattaneo.

Sekaran, U. (2000). *Research methods for business* (3rd ed). New York, NY: John Wiley & Sons, Inc.

Sekaran, U., & Bougie, R. (2016). *Research methods for business: A skill building approach*. London: John Wiley & Sons.

Shane, S., & Venkataraman, S. (2000). The promise of entrepreneurship as a field of research. *Academy of Management Review, 25*(1), 217–226. doi:doi.org/10.5465/amr.2000.2791611

Shepherd, D. A. (2003). Learning from business failure: Propositions of grief recovery for the self-employed. *Academy of Management Review, 28*(2), 318–328. doi:doi.org/10.5465/amr.2003.9416377

Simon, H. A. (1987). Making management decisions: The role of intuition and emotion. *Academy of Management Perspectives, 1*(1), 57–64. doi:doi.org/10.5465/ame.1987.4275905

Slaski, M., & Cartwright, S. (2003). Emotional intelligence training and its implications for stress, health and performance. *Stress and Health, 19*(4), 233–239. doi:doi.org/10.1002/smi.979

Spearman, C. (1923). *The nature of "intelligence" and the principles of cognition*. London: Macmillan.

Spector, P. E. (1994). *Job satisfaction survey*. Tampa, FL: University of South Florida

Sternberg, R. J. (1984). Toward a triarchic theory of human intelligence. *Behavioral and Brain Sciences, 7*(2), 269–287. doi:doi.org/0140-525X/84/020269-47/$06.00

Stroe, S., Sirén, C., Shepherd, D., & Wincent, J. (2020). The dualistic regulatory effect of passion on the relationship between fear of failure and negative affect: Insights from facial expression analysis. *Journal of Business Venturing, 35*(4), 105948. doi:doi.org/10.1016/j.jbusvent.2019.105948

Sy, T., Côté, S., & Saavedra, R. (2005). The contagious leader: Impact of the leader's mood on the mood of group members, group affective tone, and group processes. *Journal of Applied Psychology, 90*(2), 295. doi:doi.org/10.1037/0021-9010.90.2.295

Thompson, B. (2004). *Exploratory and confirmatory factor analysis.* Washington, DC: American Psychological Association.

Thorndike, E. L. (1920). Intelligence examinations for college entrance. *The Journal of Educational Research, 1*(5), 329–337. doi:10.1080/00220671.19 20.10879060

Thurstone, L. L. (1938). *Primary mental abilities* (Vol. 119). Chicago, IL: University of Chicago Press.

Ucbasaran, D., Westhead, P., & Wright, M. (2009). The extent and nature of opportunity identification by experienced entrepreneurs. *Journal of Business Venturing, 24*(2), 99–115. doi:doi.org/10.1016/j.jbusvent.2008.01.008

Uhl-Bien, M., & Arena, M. (2018). Leadership for organizational adaptability: A theoretical synthesis and integrative framework. *The Leadership Quarterly, 29*(1), 89–104. doi:doi.org/10.1016/j.leaqua.2017.12.009

Van Teijlingen, E., & Hundley, V. (2002). The importance of pilot studies. *Nursing Standard (through 2013), 16*(40), 33.

Venkatraman, N., & Ramanujam, V. (1986). Measurement of business performance in strategy research: A comparison of approaches. *Academy of Management Review, 11*(4), 801–814. doi:doi.org/10.5465/amr.1986.4283976

Watson, D., Clark, L. A., & Tellegen, A. (1988). Development and validation of brief measures of positive and negative affect: The PANAS scales. *Journal of Personality and Social Psychology, 54*(6), 1063.

Wechsler, D. (1950). Cognitive, conative, and non-intellective intelligence. *American Psychologist, 5*(3), 78. doi:doi.org/10.1037/h0063112

Weiss, H. M., & Cropanzano, R. (1996). Affective Events Theory: A theoretical discussion of the structure, causes and consequences of affective experiences at work. In B. M. Staw & L. L. Cummings (Eds.), *Research in organizational behavior: An annual series of analytical essays and critical reviews* (Vol. 18, pp. 1–74). New York, NY: Elsevier Science/JAI Press.

Welpe, I. M., Spörrle, M., Grichnik, D., Michl, T., & Audretsch, D. B. (2012). Emotions and opportunities: The interplay of opportunity evaluation, fear, joy, and anger as antecedent of entrepreneurial exploitation. *Entrepreneurship Theory and Practice, 36*(1), 69–96. doi:doi. org/10.1111/j.1540-6520.2011.00481.x

Wiklund, J., & Shepherd, D. (2003). Knowledge-based resources, entrepreneurial orientation, and the performance of small and medium-sized businesses. *Strategic Management Journal, 24*(13), 1307–1314. doi:doi. org/10.1002/smj.360

Wolff, S. B. (2005, January 21). *Emotional competence inventory (ECI): Technical manual.* Philadelphia, PA: Hay Group.

Wong, C. S., & Law, K. S. (2002). The effects of leader and follower emotional intelligence on performance and attitude: An exploratory study. *The Leadership Quarterly, 13*(3), 243–274. doi:doi.org/10.1016/ S1048-9843(02)00099-1

Woodworth, R. S. (1940). *Psychology* (4th ed.). New York, NY: Henry Holt.

Young, P. T. (1936). *Motivation of behavior.* London: Wiley.

Zajonc, R. B. (1998). Emotions. In D. T. Gilbert, S. T. Fiske, & G. Lindzey (Eds.), *The handbook of social psychology* (pp. 591–632). New York, NY: McGraw-Hill.

Zampetaskis, L. A., Beldekos, P., & Moustakis, V. S. (2009). "Day-to-day" entrepreneurship within organizations: The role of the trait emotional intelligence and perceived organizational support. *European Management Journal, 27*, 165–175. doi:doi.org/10.1016/j.emj.2008.08.003

Zevon, M. A., & Tellegen, A. (1982). The structure of mood change: An idiographic/nomothetic analysis. *Journal of Personality and Social Psychology, 43*(1), 111–122. https://doi.org/10.1037/0022-3514.43.1.111

Zhou, J., & George, J. M. (2003). Awakening employee creativity: The role of leader emotional intelligence. *The Leadership Quarterly, 14*(4–5), 545–568. doi:doi.org/10.1016/S1048-9843(03)00051-1

INDEX